"Neil Brown's *Ending the Parent-Teen Control Battle* is an exhilarating read for anyone who lives or works with teens. You'll find a breakthrough insight on every page, from targeting the control battle and not the teens themselves, to simple fixes for reducing reactivity and negativity to stop control battles. No book on parenting teens has felt so fresh and filled with so much hard-won wisdom from decades in the consulting room as *Ending the Parent-Teen Control Battle*. Brown's book is a gift to every parent of a teen."

—**Lara Honos-Webb, PhD**, author of *The ADHD Workbook for Teens* (www.addisagift.com)

"If you have faith in yourself, your teen, and the irrepressible power of family, you've struck gold with this book. Brown will guide you step by step through 'taming the Beast' that often arises when raising adolescents while guiding them to their highest potential."

—**Edward Farrar, LMFT**, child, adolescent, and family specialist in McMinnville, OR

"As a primary care physician trusted with the intricacies of family dynamics within the office setting, this book has become an instrumental tool in helping guide my communication between parents and adolescents. It has helped me begin and execute a plan to help families find help for destroying 'the Beast' that manifests not only as emotional complaints, but also physical symptoms in both parents and teens. But more importantly, it has given me guidance as I navigate my own family dynamic. I am blessed to be the mom of my own teen! Thank you, Neil Brown, for showing me how to refocus our relationship and to stay positive. I highly recommend this book to all families entering into the teen years!"

—**Patricia Golden, DO**, medical director of Wheaton Franciscan Medical Group-Ascension Health Care Central Market Wisconsin, and member of the American Academy of Family Practice

"Neil Brown's book cuts through the cultural myths that have left parents of adolescents shackled and confused. In clear, easy-to-understand steps, he creates road maps toward solutions and results. This book is a great resource for parents of 12- to 18-year-olds."

—**Joe Newman, MA**, author of *Raising Lions*

"As a marriage and family therapist for over thirty-six years, I have worked with adolescents and their families, and have encountered the control battles so insightfully described in Neil Brown's *Ending the Parent-Teen Control Battle*. I thoroughly enjoyed reading the book for its clear language, warm tone, and pragmatic content. The metaphor of 'the Beast' gives therapists and parents a common language to describe the problem ('feeding the Beast') and implement solutions ('starving the Beast'). The section about the adolescent brain is also particularly helpful in describing and understanding adolescent behavior. I believe that this book can become an essential tool for therapists as well as parents in promoting effective ways to support and guide adolescents."

—**Carmen Arriaga, LMFT, RN**, marriage and family therapist and registered nurse in private practice, and adjunct faculty at Santa Clara University's graduate program in counseling psychology

"With diligence, creativity, and an unwavering desire to help families, Neil Brown has gifted both therapists and parents with this expert book. Engagingly written, it offers a fresh look at the 'parent-teen control battle,' and clearly outlines a method for resolving it. Featuring a number of clinical vignettes, the book is not only practical, but illuminating and inspiring as well. From a psychiatrist's standpoint, I particularly appreciate how the book addresses certain physiological considerations in teens. Recent neuropsychological findings shed light on the development of the teenage brain, further reframing and 'normalizing' some of the challenges families face. Along with the methods set forth, this knowledge helps to ease the despair of both parents and teens caught in seemingly endless struggles. As a compassionate, widely respected therapist, Neil Brown provides both hope and direction to families seeking affirmative change."

—**Andrew Kumasaka, MD**, psychiatrist in private practice

"Identifying 'the Beast' in your home will turn your family around. It was insightful to see how parents often inadvertently contribute to the control battle. It is invaluable to understand that the parent's role is to guide by providing structure with a positive tone while allowing teens to own their behavior and earn their privileges. Parenting can be enjoyable and rewarding again. A strong recommendation to my patients. A must-read for all families."

—**Martha Sandoval, MD**, family medicine, Palo Alto Medical Foundation

"As a pediatrician and father, I found this book to be of the utmost importance for understanding the health and well-being of families. When addressing any family problem, from seemingly minor health issues to a devastating disease, we, as physicians, must acknowledge the unique dynamics of the family system. Everything I do as a pediatrician and parent involves these dynamics. The ideas from this book will enable the reader to clearly understand challenging dynamics with easy-to-understand advice to create healthy parent-teen relationships. I highly recommend this book for parents, therapists, educators, and healthcare practitioners working with adolescents."

> —**Garry Crummer, MD**, integrative pediatrics practitioner in Santa Cruz, CA, and former clinical professor of pediatrics at the University of California, San Diego School of Medicine's Division of Community Pediatrics

"*Ending the Parent-Teen Control Battle* defines a purposeful and mindful path through the often volatile minefield of life with a defiant teen. Neil Brown's strong, experienced, and always-to-the-point voice has helped our family clarify our problematic journey with our teen grandson. His book brings organization and rational thought to an often messy, disorderly family dynamic. It reminds parents to envision our child as his best self, and helps us to become our best parenting selves. Simply put, this book has provided us the knowledge, hope, and courage to greet each new teen-parenting day."

> —**Margaret Wilson**, custodial grandparent

"Written with a profound respect for both teens and parents, Neil Brown traverses the rocky road of adolescence with wisdom and practicality. As a family therapist, I have experienced parent-teen control battles as one of the most challenging issues that many families face. This guide book is filled with realistic and relatable scenarios, extremely effective tools, and relationship-enhancing strategies. Parents, as well as therapists, will come away with a deep understanding of the stages and brain changes of adolescence, the potential pitfalls of parenting, and concrete steps to successfully navigate the challenges of raising a teen."

> —**Andrea Wachter, LMFT**, psychotherapist, coauthor of *Mirror, Mirror on the Wall* and *The Don't Diet, Live It! Workbook*; and author of *Getting Over Overeating for Teens*

"Neil Brown has written a wonderful book for parents of teens. In conversational language, Neil highlights the importance of parental emotional awareness and control, attention to their teen's temperament, and an unafraid approach to being straight with kids about their behavior and their need to earn privileges through behavioral control and honesty. By focusing on the battle for control, Brown helps parents avoid giving up and avoid excessively labeling and blaming their teen.... It is certainly a book I could recommend to parents of teens in my practice and in my community."

> —**John Sargent, MD**, professor of psychiatry and pediatrics, and director of the Division of Child and Adolescent Psychiatry at Tufts University School of Medicine

"Reflecting decades of experience as a therapist, this easy-to-read book by Neil Brown will be a valuable resource for parents. *Ending the Parent-Teen Control Battle* provides both smart analysis of a troublesome dynamic that often creeps into relations between parents and teens, and very clear advice on how to either avoid it or get on top if it when it develops."

> —**Bonnie Fox, PhD**, professor of sociology at the University of Toronto, Canada

"As a former middle school principal, parent, and concerned educational leader, I have experienced the parent-teen control battle from all fronts: professionally, personally, and academically. When Neil Brown came to present for our middle school, his strategies for setting caring, supportive boundaries and communicating non-confrontationally with teens were instantly accessible and understandable for our parent community. This book contains practical case studies and concrete examples of behavior and language that are clear and immediately useful. Brown gives constructive advice regarding the 'developmental bridge' that we all help our teens cross as parents, educators, and support providers. Anyone supporting healthy relationships and communication with teenagers can benefit from the strategies and information this book contains."

> —**Valerie Royaltey-Quandt, EdD**, director of student services at Campbell Union High School District

ENDING THE
PARENT- TEEN
CONTROL BATTLE

Resolve the Power Struggle &
Build Trust, Responsibility & Respect

NEIL D. BROWN, LCSW

New Harbinger Publications, Inc.

Publisher's Note

NEW HARBINGER PUBLICATIONS is a registered trademark of New Harbinger Publications, Inc.

Distributed in Canada by Raincoast Books

Copyright © 2016 by Neil D. Brown
New Harbinger Publications, Inc.
5674 Shattuck Avenue
Oakland, CA 94609
www.newharbinger.com

Cover design by Amy Shoup; Interior design by Michele Waters-Kermes; Acquired by Jess O'Brien; Edited by Rona Bernstein

---

Library of Congress Cataloging-in-Publication Data

Names: Brown, Neil D., author.
Title: Ending the parent-teen control battle : resolve the power struggle and build trust, responsibility, and respect / Neil D. Brown, LCSW ; foreword by Donald T. Saposnek, PhD.
Description: Oakland, CA : New Harbinger Publications, Inc., [2016] | Includes bibliographical references.
Identifiers: LCCN 2016014552 (print) | LCCN 2016023706 (ebook) | ISBN 9781626254244 (pbk. : alk. paper) | ISBN 9781626254251 (pdf e-book) | ISBN 9781626254268 (epub) | ISBN 9781626254251 (PDF e-book) | ISBN 9781626254268 (ePub)
Subjects: LCSH: Parent and teenager. | Parenting.
Classification: LCC HQ799.15 .B76 2016 (print) | LCC HQ799.15 (ebook) | DDC 306.874--dc23
LC record available at https://lccn.loc.gov/2016014552

Printed in the United States of America

23   22   21

10   9   8   7   6   5   4

DEDICATION

I dedicate this book to
Milton, Lydia, Paul, and Carl.

Contents

Foreword

The late 1960s and early 1970s changed the professional paradigm for some of us therapists as to how we view psychopathology, moving from conceptualizing the "problem" of a symptomatic individual as being *inside the person* to seeing the problem as existing *within relationships* (i.e., between two or more people). The seminal work of family therapists Virginia Satir, Jay Haley, Salvador Minuchin, and others brought a veritable renaissance of family systems thinking into the world of psychotherapy.

Neil Brown has combined his experience as a seasoned therapist for adolescents with his early training in Minuchin's approach as a structural family therapist to create a model for understanding and treating struggling adolescents through a family systems perspective. In this book, he details how parents (and therapists) can see the adolescent's problem as essentially a *family* problem, and resolve the problem through a reconstruction of the family interactions. He uses the techniques of *positive reframing* (shifting from a negative to a positive view of the people and their intentions) and of shifting the hierarchy of power from the teen being in charge of the family to the parents being in charge, but only of themselves. This results in the paradoxical outcome of the adolescent taking charge of him- or herself in a more responsible way, guided implicitly by the parents asserting their power through powerlessness (nonstruggling).

There is a calm, caring, but firm, assertive, and respectful feeling to Neil's approach. If the family makes the shift, all members wind up showing deep respect for each other, which creates greater harmony among the family members. In attempts to lead the adolescent toward accepting responsibility, Neil encourages the parents to accept their own responsibility in maintaining the *Control Battle* ("feeding the Beast"). Not only does this shift the tone from blaming others to assuming one's own responsibility, it also models for the teen how to do this, while allowing the parents to keep a positive image of their teen, as they are no longer encumbered by their anger and disappointment about their teen's behavior. This, then, allows the teens the psychological breathing space to rethink who they are and what they really want as goals for themselves. It also, paradoxically, lets them appreciate their parents, who they previously saw as oppressors of their freedom.

The late family therapist Jay Haley described the essential developmental task for teens as "being prepared to leave home." Neil's approach gives teens that very preparatory opportunity: the chance to shift from being a surly, procrastinating, goal-less, passive, disengaged individual with a negative attitude toward life to being a more energized, productive, goal-focused, active, and engaged individual with a positive and hopeful attitude toward life, and with a more tolerant and loving attitude toward his or her parents.

In recent years, psychotherapy has relentlessly been forced back into the "problem is within the individual" model, driven largely by political power of the health insurance industry and by Big Pharma's enormous influence over how practitioners practice; the "standard of care" has become the promoting of a limited number of, individual, psychotherapeutic interventions, and the use of medications whenever possible. The primary model for insurance reimbursement requires diagnosing a single "patient" and seeing that patient in sessions alone. As such, family therapy (for which insurance companies pay therapists less than they do for individual therapy, or nothing at all) is rapidly becoming a lost art.

Kudos to Neil for continuing to respect the power of the family system for creating and for resolving the struggles of adolescents. In fact, I remember Neil telling me some 30 years ago that he found it peculiar that the DSM (*Diagnostic and Statistical Manual of Mental Disorders*) has an individual diagnosis of oppositional defiant disorder, when, by definition, the "disorder" (which presumably would be inside the individual) would require that the adolescent oppose someone else (essentially making it a relationship disorder!).

Unlike other parenting books, which simply rely on crafting more punitive, top-down approaches for "fixing" the behavior of teens, *Ending the Parent-Teen Control Battle* embraces the essence of family theory and family therapy as the most effective, comprehensive approach—an approach that builds in maintenance of the family's positive changes. Without such a systems approach, relational changes are typically short-lived.

Neil's book will be well-received by its readership. It is written in a clear, friendly, and informative style, with good examples of typical family control battles, and with sample scripted language that parents can immediately use to begin reshaping their negative family interactions into positive resolutions of conflict. Reading and fully implementing the guidelines in this book will certainly help you stop "feeding the Beast." My best wishes to the readers.

—Donald T. Saposnek, PhD
　　Clinical Child Psychologist and Family Therapist
　　Department of Psychology,
　　　University of California, Santa Cruz

Why I Wrote This Book

Long before I went to graduate school, I knew I wanted to be a family therapist. I had been working as a teacher in a school for children with developmental delays in southern Colorado and I discovered something amazing. When we drove out to the students' distant rural homes, met with their parents, and told them how much we enjoyed their kids, it created a profound difference in how the children performed. They went from defeated, depressed, unmotivated students to happy, engaged kids. I knew then and there that a magical transformative power existed within families, and I wanted to learn how to tap into it.

To this day I am an active student in the field of family therapy, and although I've studied the work of many of the greats in our field, I have focused mostly on structural family therapy and the work of renowned psychiatrist, Salvador Minuchin and his colleagues. In his book *Families and Family Therapy*, Minuchin (1974) described the repetitive patterns of behavior within families that underscore either healthy functioning or potential problems. He documented the importance of a well-functioning hierarchy in families in order for children to grow up with appropriate structure. He used a variety of techniques to break the problematic family patterns and replace them with new and healthier patterns. I received training in this model at the Philadelphia Child Guidance Clinic (PCGC) under Minuchin's directorship. Later, when I was the program manager for an outpatient adolescent counseling center, one of the PCGC trainers, child psychiatrist John Sargent, trained our therapists in this approach.

Whether I studied structural family therapy or any other family therapy approach, one thing was clear: patterns of behavior within families are powerful and enduring. The art and practice of family therapy is based on helping families transform ongoing negative patterns into positive ones. There are volumes written on the subject, but there is simply no easy answer about how to accomplish this. With 38 years of experience, I now have much more success transforming these patterns than I used to, but it's taken a lot of practice, trial and error, training, and commitment. And it still isn't easy.

You may have noticed the recent proliferation of books on the subject of parenting in general, and more specifically on parenting teenagers. The modern era of the subject of parenting goes back perhaps to notable pediatrician Benjamin Spock, who in 1946 published *The Common Sense Book of Baby and Child Care*, one of the top selling books of all time. Prior to Spock, behaviorists advised that responding to infants' requests would spoil them and leave them ill-prepared for the real world. I wonder to this day if my mother would have picked me up when I cried as an infant had she not read that book! Since that time, the growth and development of this field has given parents valuable information to better understand their children and teens and learn strategies to help them grow in healthy ways. It has also created a forum for discussion about our values related to raising kids.

But too often this parenting advice does not actually address the serious struggles that many families have. The reason for this has everything to do with the power of persistence in relationships and relationship patterns. In struggling families, even if the primary struggle is between one parent and only one of several kids, *everyone* in the family will become involved in, and affected by, the struggle. That's how powerful and pervasive relationship patterns can be.

So I decided to write a book to help parents understand the power of negative relationship patterns in families and learn how to change them. Because childhood and adolescence offer such different challenges, and because these negative relationship patterns so often emerge during the teen years, I have focused this book on families raising teenagers.

Since I've spent my career studying and working with these relationship patterns, I've become quite adept at seeing them. When I first meet a family, I gather information about each family member and discover their unique strengths; then I ask about the problem the family has come to talk with me about. After a while, the family members begin to interact with each other in their natural way, and the relationship patterns emerge. That's where we find the opportunity to create real and lasting change, transforming the negative relationship pattern into a positive one. I've come to call this negative relationship pattern the *Control Battle*. And the Control Battle is what this book is all about.

You'll discover that I have created a personification of the control battle that I refer to as the *Beast*. I've chosen to do this at the risk of sounding corny or gimmicky, because the enduring negative pattern in families is the real culprit. It's the real cause of the pain and suffering that goes on. It's not the kid, it's not the parent—it's the pattern; and it's so real for me that it seems to come alive, almost as an entity in itself. When we personify the control battle, it helps us understand how real and powerful it is, and it also helps us see that it's this *Beast* who is the enemy—not any one member of our family.

Early in my career, in my efforts to help the adults take charge in families where teens were acting out and being unaccountable, I often emphasized the need for a strong parental voice accompanied by strong action. My goal to support parental authority was worthy, but my tactics tended to strengthen the hidden control battle that lived between parents and kids. Later I became a father myself, and this brought out my softer, gentler side. Little by little, as I gained experience both as a therapist and as a father, I learned that a nurturing hierarchy could be established and maintained far more effectively with love and support than with a heavy handed, authoritarian tone.

Over the course of my career, I've gained valuable insights into the specific elements that create and support control battles, as well as some effective ways to end them. In fact, this has been my life's work. I use this knowledge and experience to help the families I see, and I've shared this information with countless middle and high school parents, speaking in school auditoriums for many years. And now I'm sharing it with you.

This book is not a substitute for counseling or therapy, but it can help you decide if counseling is needed, guide you toward the right kind of help for your situation, and augment and reinforce any professional help you're receiving. To help you determine whether counseling is needed, please visit http://www.newharbinger.com/34244 and read the online chapter "Should I Consider Counseling?"

As we'll talk about in chapter 2, "Adolescence, an Invitation to the Control Battle," the teen years are the bridge between childhood and young adulthood. Parenting a teenager must be approached in a way that facilitates this transition. While this book is designed to help parents and teens already locked in a control battle, it will also give you the knowledge and skills you need to help your teen do the growing he or she needs to do and avoid the pitfalls of future control battles.

What will you find in these pages? Part 1 of *Ending the Parent-Teen Control Battle* provides an in-depth understanding of what the Control Battle is and how it develops. Part 2 gives you the specific skills to end the Control Battle, and Part 3 addresses advanced applications for specific common issues. Although there are many psychological conditions that can invite control battles, I've focused on just a few that I most commonly see in my practice. Two chapters in Part 3 were heavily influenced by two important professional relationships I've developed, which deserve mention.

I met John Fleming, the owner and director of Developmental Learning Solutions of Santa Cruz and San Jose, California, in the early 1990s. John is an educational therapist whose clinic assesses, diagnoses, and provides a host of resources for kids with learning disabilities. Prior to meeting and working with John, I had been struggling to help certain kids and families who were locked in a control battle around schoolwork. When John and I began working together, I came to see that when these kids' learning needs were assessed, understood, and addressed—in a way that utilized the ending the control battle model—struggling kids and families were able to get back onto the road to health and success. I realized I had a powerful new response to the control battle that would help dismantle it. You can learn more about this in chapter 9, "Learning Disabilities and ADHD."

Another important professional relationship I developed was with Mark Burdick, an educational and clinical psychologist who specializes in therapeutic placements for at-risk adolescents and young adults. Prior to meeting and working with Mark, I had a bias against placing teens with seriously destructive behaviors in programs away from their homes. After all, from my perspective as a family theorist and therapist, how does sending a kid with behavior problems to a program do anything to change the negative relationship patterns in the family?

Through many conversations, I learned that Mark strongly agrees with me that to be effective, the manner in which teenagers are placed, along with the programs themselves, needs to help *families* change negative relationship patterns into positive ones. This way, the teens can be safe while both they and their families receive the help and support they need to be successful when the teenagers return home. I also learned that different programs are best suited for certain kids, and finding the right program makes all the difference in the success of the outcome. There is more on this subject in chapter 11, "When Your Teen Is Seriously Out of Control."

As an adjunct to this book, I have also written a chapter for your teen to read called "For Teens Only," which you will find online at http://www.newharbinger.com/34244. This chapter will provide your teen with an understanding of what a healthy path forward for a teenager really is. It includes much of the information you'll find in this book, but in terms that are geared toward teenagers.

For you to benefit most from this book, it will be important to start at the beginning and read consecutively through chapter 7, "Self-Esteem and Happiness." That way you'll have a strong understanding of the ending the parent-teen control battle model. Then, if you want to go ahead to a chapter that focuses on an application of the model to a specific circumstance, you will be well prepared to absorb that material. Once you have read the first seven chapters and your teen has read "For Teens Only," you'll be ready to sit down together, discuss what you've read and how it applies to your family, and commit to making healthy changes. You might ask each other these questions:

> Are there ways in which we have a Control Battle? Do we have a Beast in our relationship?

> If we do have one, what are the one or two things we could each do that would "starve the Beast"?

> If we don't have one, what are the one or two things we need to keep doing, or do more of, to keep the Beast away?

So if you're at your wits' end and tired of the constant struggle with your teen, be assured that the powerful insights, interventions, and tools you will need to move forward are all right here. This book will help take the pressure off you to get your teen to perform and will put that responsibility squarely in the hands of your teen—which is where it belongs. With this important shift, you will be able to build a relationship of trust and respect and thoroughly enjoy these teen years before launching your son or daughter into the world of young adulthood.

UNDERSTANDING THE CONTROL BATTLE

CHAPTER 1

What Is the Control Battle? (Meet the Beast)

Just think of it—here we are with all of our good intentions, wanting nothing more than to help our kids be happy and successful. And our kids want only to be happy and successful as well. And yet, everything we do, and everything *they* do, gets distorted and turned into something ugly and counterproductive. How can this be?

Simple things, like getting your teenager to do homework, do a chore, be nice to his or her sibling, or simply be home on time, can seem overwhelming. Just getting your kid out of bed and off to school in the morning can be an ordeal that saps the pleasure out of the day. Sometimes the problems are far more severe, such as those involving crime, drug abuse, and other dangerous behaviors. You've read some excellent parenting books and applied the methods, but to no avail. You may have sought counseling for yourself and your teenager with little lasting improvement.

At some point you may question whether things will ever get better. "Is it hopeless? Is this how life is going to be now? Is my teenager impossible? Am I a bad parent?" And the answer is—no! Your situation is not hopeless, your teenager is not impossible, and you are not a bad parent.

What I am going to share with you is how to recognize a pattern of interaction that may be happening in your family, the pattern I have named the *parent-teen control battle*. I'll show you what the control battle is all about and how developmental shifts in adolescence contribute to its creation. You'll develop an understanding of the difference between typical power struggles and a control battle, and how you can be truly reempowered as a parent. And as you reclaim your role as an effective parent, you will learn how to empower your adolescent to grow and invest all that amazing adolescent energy in a healthy direction.

While control battles can exist for parents of children from toddlerhood through—and including—adulthood, this book is designed specifically for parents of middle- and high-school-age teenagers. The developmental tasks and challenges are unique for this age group, so the approaches to parenting without control battles, and to ending control battles when they do develop, must be unique and specific as well.

Parenting Styles

There are many styles of parenting within a wide range of cultural and personal norms, most of which can work quite well. You probably know parents who are very strict, and parents who are quite lenient. You know families in which religion is very important, and families in which sports, music, or the arts are encouraged. I'm sure you're aware of teens from these different styles of families who are just fine, and others who are struggling. Strict parents can have problems with their teens, as can parents with a more relaxed style. Religious and nonreligious families alike may have well-behaved and successful teenagers, yet they may experience challenging and difficult situations with their teens as well.

Additionally, many parents feel the pressure to be "a perfect parent." Let me reassure you that nobody parents perfectly. When it comes to raising kids, we've all done things that mental health professionals would advise against doing. We all get angry, and most of us raise our voices sometimes. We may lecture ineffectively, punish our kids for doing something they didn't know was wrong, overindulge, oversupport, underindulge, and undersupport. We give our teenagers guidance and set limits when they would probably be better off making decisions and learning about consequences on their own. Or we fail to step in to offer guidance or set limits when they truly need us to.

This is ordinary family life! Despite their parents' human imperfections, kids can and do thrive, growing up to lead happy and successful lives.

I am not trying to convince you that nothing we do makes any difference, nor am I trying to encourage you to be thoughtless as a parent. I *am* saying that there is a wide range of values and approaches that can be equally effective, and being a perfect parent is impossible.

So let's be clear: there is no "right kind of family," there is no such thing as a perfect family, and all families have problems. So if you are struggling with your teenager, please don't decide that you are a bad parent or that you have a bad kid. Let's just decide that you are a parent looking for a better way to understand and deal with problems you're having with your teenager. And that's a good thing.

Now let's look at this phenomenon that I call the Control Battle.

Some Parent-Teen Struggles Are Healthy

It's important to acknowledge and accept that to a certain extent the parent-teen power struggle is natural. It's part of how kids grow up and how change happens in families to accommodate teen development. Kids are often testing limits, and parents respond either by reaffirming those limits or by accepting that perhaps it's time to change a limit. For instance, you agree that your fourteen-year-old son can go to a party, but you want him home at the usual curfew of 11:00 p.m. Your son gets upset and pleads with you to extend the curfew to 1:00 a.m. because that's how late the other kids are allowed to stay, and he "feels like a baby" having to leave the party early when everyone else is still having fun. You relinquish previously-set expectations and agree to a compromise of midnight, but you are somewhat concerned. You know your son needs his sleep to do well the next day, and you realize that you're setting a new precedent. But you figure that you'll see how it goes because you don't want your son to feel embarrassed about being treated as less mature than his friends.

The way this agreement was made involved a certain amount of emotional upset, arguing, and negotiating. There is a natural push/pull that goes on between kids and parents that is common, normal, and important. Of course we want these parent-teen struggles to be as respectful and reasonable as possible, but they do tend to become emotional. The good news is, even with some amount of kid-parent emotion and conflict, our teens can still do well and the parent-teen relationship can still be healthy.

Some Parent-Teen Struggles Are Control Battles

Yet sometimes it seems as if nothing we do is working. It seems we have only two options: fight with our teen or let things go. If we try to discuss things, it turns into an argument. If we put our foot down, it provokes a crisis. If we do nothing, our son or daughter will simply fail. And it's been going on way too long, sapping the fun and energy out of the whole family. If this sounds familiar, you are experiencing the phenomenon of the *Control Battle*.

A parent-teen control battle is the chronic struggle between a parent and adolescent who are each engaged in a constant attempt to get what they want. The parent is attempting to get the teen to behave in a certain way—to do chores or homework, to stop fighting with siblings, stop using drugs, stop staying out all night, or whatever it may be. The teen is attempting to resist parental control, struggling to get or do what he wants.

Caught in the Clutches of the Beast

The Control Battle is a self-perpetuating and destructive pattern of interaction. It has a momentum all its own. Elements of the control battle are going on even when the parent and teen are not directly engaged. Before the parent even begins to interact with the teen, both will anticipate a negative response. The parent will likely expect push-back and anger from the teen. The teen will likely expect the parent to be critical, disapproving, or controlling.

In control battle–based relationships, these negative expectations drive the relationship. Even when parents—or teenagers—intentionally offer their best communication, hoping to positively influence the relationship, any happy result is likely to be short-lived as the negative relationship pattern quickly returns. This is because control battle–based relationships go beyond any cause-and-effect explanation. The control battle phenomenon is interactive and complex, with each person affected by the other, and ultimately the momentum of the control battle itself affects them both. It is this quality of the control battle, the negative and destructive momentum it builds, that makes it so difficult to transcend and heal.

A control battle can be so powerful that it often overwhelms our best intentions and renders us completely ineffective and helpless. We can think of the control battle as a diabolical, cynical creature who loves to distort reality, create havoc, turn the simple into the complex, turn the easy into the difficult, and take the pleasure out of our lives. I see this creature as ugly and menacing, like Jabba the Hutt from Star Wars. This creature lives off of our negativity, our doubt, our fears, our frustration, and our anger. When we parent within the control battle paradigm, we feed the Beast. The more we feed it, the bigger it bloats up, and this fiend

13

just gets more and more powerful. When we operate *outside* the control battle paradigm, the Beast starves, loses power, weakens, and dies a natural death.

The powerful advantage of this perspective is that it changes the target of our efforts from our teen to the control battle itself. And since we can't fight what we can't see, by visualizing the phenomenon as an entity, we can see what we're up against. We then gain the opportunity to wage an effective fight against it, render it powerless, and get it out of our lives. Our job is to starve the Beast and end the control battle.

As a therapist, I have learned that no problem or issue can be addressed successfully if the attempt to solve it takes place within the context of the control battle. It matters little whether the issue revolves around chores, schoolwork, curfew, or your teen's disrespectful communications. And it's just as pertinent with issues of depression, substance abuse, and aggressive behavior. In order to create lasting change, families must learn and understand the secrets of the control battle and take the critical steps to end it.

Let's look at one example of a mother-son control battle.

Cameron

Cameron is an eighth grade boy who lives with his mother and younger brother and visits his father on weekends. Cameron has never loved doing schoolwork, but now it's become an almost constant battle for his mother to get him to complete his assignments. What he really wants to do is skateboard and play video games. His teachers have tried to work with him, but he seems to want no part of their help. Recently Cameron has started hanging out with other kids who do poorly in school and are known to smoke cigarettes and marijuana.

Cameron's pattern is to put off schoolwork and do it only when it can't be delayed any longer, usually with a lot of prompting and support from his mother. Typically Mom will start off nicely, asking Cameron what work he has to do, and Cameron will be evasive, until Mom pushes through his hedging, pins him down, and gets him going.

Mom is understandably concerned that Cameron isn't growing up to manage his responsibilities and now is starting to "go downhill." And after working all day, making dinner, supporting her younger son, and then having to struggle with Cameron, Mom is feeling more than frustrated; she is feeling hopeless and burned out.

Mom decides to bring Cameron to a counselor, who says Cameron is depressed and sad that his father isn't more involved in his life. This confirms Mom's thinking. But what is she supposed to do?

The counselor recommends a behavior plan in which Cameron can earn or lose certain privileges based on how he completes his work. This sounds reasonable to Mom, and Cameron doesn't object, but when it comes down to it, it is still Mom doing the work to get Cameron to do his work and earn his privileges. When she revokes a privilege, Cameron fights with her and promises to do his work, and Mom, who is thin on energy to begin with, often accepts his promises and moves on, only to have Cameron continue to put his work off. When Mom does take away his privileges, this seems to have no effect. Cameron just broods, is rude to his mother, and acts mean to his younger brother.

Cameron's mother is concerned that there is more going on here than the act of taking away privileges can address. Does Cameron simply have the same genes as his irresponsible father? Perhaps Cameron has accepted his father's view that the divorce was Mom's fault. In fact, Mom has worried about Cameron ever since the divorce. She worries that taking his privileges away will cause him to feel he's been abandoned by both parents and make the situation even worse. So things continue much this same way, within the pattern of their control battle—Mom coaxing, pushing, and finally punishing in an attempt to help Cameron succeed, and Cameron avoiding and resisting. Nothing has changed and they remain firmly in the grasp of the Beast.

As frustrating and perhaps even hopeless as the situation with Cameron and his mother seems to be, if we were to zero in on the control battle, help Mom and Cameron understand the elements supporting it, and help them take the critical steps to end it, Cameron would find himself back on the path to success, and Mom would feel empowered, effective, and able to enjoy parenting her son again.

Control battles can take many forms. They can be loud, soft, obvious, or subtle. But when parents are engaged in a control battle with their kids, they feel frustrated, helpless, and sometimes hopeless. Everything, it seems, turns into a fight, a constant struggle. Imagine the feeling of having your car stuck in the mud on the side of the road. If you step on the gas, you go nowhere—you only sink deeper. If you don't step on the gas, you just sit there feeling helpless, resisting the temptation to step on the gas. It's that feeling of futility that is so painful. Parents want so much to help, yet they feel as if their teenager has rendered them completely helpless!

The Destructive Impact of the Control Battle

Control battles don't only feel bad in the moment; they can have a long-lasting negative impact on individuals and families. They undermine healthy social and emotional development in teens. Instead of putting energy into developing their strengths and improving their weaknesses, teens throw their efforts into resisting control, thereby impeding their own personal growth. Instead of learning how to manage their responsibilities, their feelings, and their attitudes, they work at avoiding responsibilities, indulging their negative feelings, and cultivating a bad attitude.

Destructive behaviors can include underachievement or failure at school, substance abuse, self-cutting, extreme diets or overeating, perfectionism, becoming either a chronic victim or a bully, and more. The more intense and long-lasting the control battle is, the more serious the impact will be on a teen's development.

Not only do control battles negatively impact kids, they often lead to parental burnout, too. After all, when we put a majority of our effort into something that continually fails, that's a formula for burnout. And burnout must be taken seriously. It can result in fatigue, insomnia, impaired concentration and attention, illness, anxiety, and depression.

The family is a social ecological system, so any stress that impacts one part of the family affects all the other parts as well. When the family's emotional resources are being consumed in a control battle, there will be fewer resources available for other people and activities. Control battles can negatively impact a parental couple's relationship and can take quality time and attention away from brothers and sisters, who come to resent their sibling or their parents who are devoting so much energy to that sibling. The other kids in the family may feel less important since their "troubled" sibling is getting the lion's share of the attention. They may start acting out or developing negative symptoms themselves; or, conversely, they may feel undue pressure to be "good" in order to reduce the stress in the family.

Think of a teen's development as a line plotted on a graph. There will be times when the growth is obvious and the line is steep, as well as times when growth is less obvious and the line is flatter. But to be healthy, the overall direction must be upward. When a teen is in chronic conflict, the line starts heading down, rather than moving up the way it should. The longer this continues, and the farther the teen falls behind in development, the more difficult it becomes to catch up.

Personal development, for better or worse, has a momentum that tends to perpetuate itself. If the direction is up, that is, toward positive improvement, the momentum will be upward. If the direction is down, the momentum continues downward in a negative expression. It is this momentum that makes change so difficult. Think of the momentum of a train going down the track. Once that train gets going, it's not easy to stop, let alone reverse. Even after the conductor puts on the brakes, the train will still be a long way down the tracks before it stops. In order to change direction, it must first slow down, make the shift, and gradually accelerate until it has a good head of steam going in the other direction.

The same thing is true when it comes to reversing the momentum of a control battle. In addition to using the right strategy, reversing a control battle will require sustained effort. Fortunately, there is an essential aspect of the control battle in which the train analogy breaks down: The train doesn't care which direction it's going. With people, there is a natural striving for growth. In a healthy situation we tend to want to improve ourselves, to love and be loved, to achieve, to feel esteemed, and to contribute. Even your teenager, who may seem bent upon sabotaging these efforts, has the natural inclination toward improvement. When you take steps to end the control battle and set a clear path forward, you have every reason to have faith that your son or daughter will be eventually heading back on the right track.

So are you in a control battle with your teen? To help you answer that question, please go to http://www.newharbinger.com /34244 and take the simple survey called "Is It a Control Battle?"

CHAPTER 2

Adolescence, an Invitation to the Control Battle

I f you are a pretty talented parent and have managed to avoid building a control battle–based relationship with your younger children, nice going! Like the rest of us, you probably get into it with your kids from time to time, but if you haven't engaged in a chronic control battle, you're doing great. Yet even if you've done well up until the teen years, adolescence can be, and often is, a game changer. Let's take a look at what's behind it.

Essentially, adolescence is that transitional period of development that bridges childhood to young adulthood. As adolescents, our kids are no longer children, and, as you surely have noticed, they're not exactly adults either! They are learning to become their own persons, increasingly able to function socially, emotionally, and economically independent from their parents. This is truly an amazing time of metamorphosis, when our children are opening their wings and learning to fly. The ultimate goal is that you and your child, now a teenager, stay lovingly connected forever. What's important now, as our sons and daughters travel through adolescence, is to gradually shift our relationship with them from one of strict parental accountability toward one of more relaxed friendship and mentoring. Yet there are many factors that keep the crossing of this developmental bridge from progressing smoothly. Some huge physiological changes take place during adolescence to support the behavioral changes required for the transition from childhood to adulthood, and for many of us, it's not a very smooth time.

Physiologically, and in many ways socially, adolescence begins at age twelve and extends into the early twenties. Full maturation doesn't occur for women until around age twenty-three, and age twenty-four or twenty-five for men. But for the purposes of this book, we'll refer to the period from after high school to age twenty-four as young adulthood, and divide adolescence into three stages.

The Three Stages of Adolescence

Early adolescence includes twelve- to fourteen-year-olds; middle adolescence, fifteen-year-olds; and late adolescence, sixteen- to eighteen-year-olds. To visualize this developmental journey, think of your child as taking a trip over an arched footbridge. As young people leave the land of childhood, they step onto the footbridge. In this early stage, they can't yet see over the curved top of the bridge to the land of adulthood, but they can look to the crest of the bridge and see the teen years ahead, and they know that's where they're going, up the footbridge to become teenagers themselves. These young adolescents look back with mixed emotions, grieving as they leave their childhoods behind, and steeling themselves for the journey ahead.

The middle adolescents have reached the top of the bridge. They have come to a place from where they can now see both sides—where they came from and where they're going—but both of these places seem far away. They're right in the middle, where they know they're no longer in the land of childhood, but they aren't ready to enter the land of young adulthood, either.

Late adolescents are on the farther side of the bridge and are not looking back at their childhoods as much. They can see the land of young adulthood ahead, and that is now their point of focus.

Each of these adolescent stages presents unique and important challenges and opportunities. Let's take a look at what's involved.

Early Adolescence

The drive to move away from one's family and toward one's peer group characterizes kids in early adolescence. When they were younger, their friends tended to be simply their classmates or neighbors. Now, as middle schoolers, our kids align with, and seek social acceptance from, other kids and peer groups, and create identities separate from their families. You might find that there are times when they behave as they always did as children, and that they still value many of the things they loved as children. And then there will be times that they hate being reminded of their childhood likes and routines. "That's stupid, I hate that," they might say in response to something they once enjoyed, including playing with their brothers and sisters. Now their younger siblings are "too babyish," and they can't tolerate being around them. They reject what we have to say about how to dress and what does or doesn't look good on them. You'll notice kids in this age group wearing clothes that you think look ridiculous on them, but as long as it's what the other kids are wearing, they're happy.

Kids are pulling away from parents at the same time that they remain highly dependent on them both emotionally and functionally. Don't believe it when they act like they don't need your love and emotional support any longer; they do! There's a good book by Anthony E. Wolf (2002) called *Get Out of My Life, but First Could You Drive Me and Cheryl to the Mall?* This title perfectly characterizes the tension between young teens' desire for independence and the reality of their dependence, humorously and beautifully. It's

21

easy to see how control battles can develop quite easily during this phase of development.

For our younger teens, pushing back against their parents and their parents' expectations is part of how they begin to separate, and parents might naturally react to this as disrespect. Many parents will be confused by what feels like a sudden change in their child's behavior. They will have heard all the stories about how kids change during adolescence, but might have thought it would be magically different for them because they've always had such a close relationship with *their* kid. So naturally they are shocked when their previously delightful child pulls away with all the typical disagreeable behaviors.

Early adolescence is a time when kids need to manage their educational responsibilities more independently. Beginning in the sixth grade, young teens have different teachers for different subjects and must learn to adjust to their varied expectations. It can be very difficult for parents to gain insight into how their young teens are doing and whether there are problems brewing. Teachers have different approaches for communicating with parents, and there can be a delay between what's going on with the teen and when the parents find out about it. Kids who have underdeveloped organizational skills, have learning issues, or are not very motivated or responsible in general will need parental support at a time when they are more reluctant than ever to accept that support. So when kids hit this developmental stage without being fully prepared for the responsibilities that go along with it, you'll find the perfect setup for the Control Battle to thrive.

Middle Adolescence

Most high school sophomores fall into the category of middle adolescence. By now they have formed their teen identities; they know their own style, their dress, their music, and their friends, and they've usually developed some confidence in their ability to be teenagers. They may have moved beyond that stage of constantly pulling away for the sake of pulling away. Fifteen-year-olds simply like what they like and want what they want. Many know the expectations and the routines and follow them quite well.

Others, having developed some mastery with independence but not yet having a strong sense of the future in front of them, seem less interested in school and parental expectations. They may have been the most delightful kids and even managed early adolescence reasonably well. But as middle teens, they begin to reject everything adult and embrace everything that goes with the word "teen." Their sense of autonomy increases. They may have older friends who are driving, so they can get rides—and they have skateboards, bikes, feet, and public transportation to take them where they want to go, independent of their parents.

It is this comfort with teen life, coupled with a lack of urgency regarding their future, that can lead many middle adolescent kids to be so challenging. Parents will work hard to keep their kids on track, while their kids resist with righteous effort. So middle adolescence is a high-risk time when it comes to entering the Control Battle. And if your fifteen-year-old is proving to be difficult, you're not alone. Hang in there and use all the skills I'll be offering you for starving the Beast, and have faith that things will get better.

Late Adolescence

In late adolescence, beginning around age sixteen, or junior year in high school, teenagers' perspective begins to change. In their quest for independence, instead of moving away from the family, the focus turns toward the future. *Where am I going? And how am I going to get there?* These are the questions looming in their minds. It might not appear as if they're thinking about that at all, given the lack of focus many late teens continue to exhibit, but believe me, they are!

It seems that for most kids, age sixteen is a magical point at which the looming reality suddenly hits home—*I'm just twenty-four short months to legal adulthood and the end of mandatory parental support!* Up until this age, it might have seemed as if life would go on, year after year, very much the same as it did the year before. Now kids can begin to see the horizon where life as they have known it will come to an end, and they will need a plan. That horizon can look very much like a cliff, and it can be quite frightening.

When teens in this stage are doing well, parent-teen relationships can go relatively smoothly. Many kids understand the basic rules and standards required of them, have in large part internalized those expectations, and function well with only a few prompts to help them stay on track. Some will need a bit more structure, and most will require guidance and support for planning their next stage in life. If they are bound for college, the process of selecting and applying to colleges is enormous. Many families benefit from using an independent college consultant to help with all this, and young people often respond better to adults other than their parents when tasks and deadlines have to be achieved. Many teens will be thinking of options other than college, or looking for some "real world" experience before they attend college. Parental support to help them think through their goals and plans and take some initial action will help them feel more grounded and confident and increase their likelihood of success.

Though you might see some important positive changes as your teen moves into later adolescence, there will be plenty of opportunities for parent-teen control battles, too. If a control battle has been going on prior to now, it can intensify when the next steps in your teen's life are not clear. And even when control battles have been avoided, older teens may be thinking they now can roam the world at will, and they can become a bit "too big for their britches." They will need their parents to reel them back in.

And then there is the phenomenon of "senioritis," that well-known disease that causes high school seniors to act as if high school is already over. They want to party and connect with each other 24/7—while they still can!

At this point, there are often many important and potentially stressful things for teens and parents to deal with—preparing for graduation, writing papers and passing tests, ordering caps and gowns, and tying up lots of other loose ends. The extra stress is enough to put parents, as well as teens, on edge.

Parent: Sweetheart, did you ever pay that fine for the lost library book? You can't graduate unless you do. They won't let you walk in the ceremony, and you know your grandparents are flying across the country to see you graduate.

Teen: That fine they expect me to pay is bogus! Nobody pays those fines. It was a stupid book and isn't worth the cost of the fine they're charging me. Don't worry about it.

Sound familiar?

So you see that there are many opportunities to enter the parent-teen control battle at this stage as well. I've often said that God makes eighteen-year-olds so obnoxious so their parents won't feel so sad when they move away!

Puberty and the Physiological Changes of Adolescence

Along with and contributing to this social-emotional transition are tremendous musculoskeletal, hormonal, and neurological changes as kids' bodies are morphing before their own and their parents' very eyes. Size and weight changes, in addition to primary and secondary sexual characteristics and functions, are developing. All of this can be quite tough on teens as well as on their parents. Hormonal changes have an enormous effect on mood and attitude, making for ups and downs that can be hard to understand or keep up with. Kids can be happy one minute, despondent or hostile the next.

The Adolescent Brain

Adolescent brains are going through a monumental transformational process, which actually accounts for more behavioral changes than any other factor. Research over the last twenty years has given us a much more sophisticated understanding of adolescent brain develoment. Like other organs, the human brain goes through an amazing period of growth until around age twenty-five, with maturity coming sooner for young women and later for young men. But the brain is not simply growing in size. It changes in ways that are unique to the stage of adolescence as it develops the characteristics that prepare teenagers for adulthood.

From the womb through pre-puberty and on into adulthood, our brains are growing and developing, creating neural connections of all kinds. A major remodeling process of these connections happens during adolescence, enabling a higher level of sophistication. This remodeling process involves a "pruning back" activity, trimming out underutilized connections and then laying down extra amounts of myelin, the substance that increases the speed of often-used connections. The net effect of this transition is that a person goes from having a brain filled with a lot of varied information in childhood to one of streamlined specialization and integration. Integration allows the many parts and functions of the brain to know what the others are doing.

Much of this integration process takes place in the prefrontal cortex, where the most significant growth in the brain occurs during adolescence. This is the most distinctly human part of the brain. It's the area that plans and organizes, modulates mood, controls impulses, and takes into account the long-term consequences of different choices—all those functions that we consider to be aspects of maturity. It is the part of the brain where abstract thinking takes place, enabling teens for the first time to see a number of options for solving problems and become aware of the many and varied ways to think about issues.

It is during this period of development that teens begin to ponder the meaning of life and understand that their parents are just people with their own ideas and ways of doing things. They begin to see that perhaps there are other reasonable ways to do things as well. It is the maturation of the prefrontal cortex that allows teens to self-reflect and to understand their own personalities, their feelings, and their emotional needs as well as the emotional needs of others.

The Dopamine Effects

Unique to adolescent neurodevelopment is a heightened release of dopamine, a neurotransmitter that drives reward-seeking behavior. In other words, teenagers may have an increased desire to seek out and do things that will make them, in the short term, feel good. Daniel Siegel (2014), in his book *Brainstorm*, explains the effects of this increased dopamine release on teen behavior. The first effect is impulsivity—adolescents simply react to the drive for pleasure before giving any real thought or evaluation to their actions.

A second effect of increased dopamine release is the tendency of teenagers to minimize the potential downsides of a behavior in favor of the upsides, or perceived gains. Say you are going out of town for a few days and you decide to trust your generally responsible sixteen-year-old daughter to stay at a friend's house. With access to your empty house, your lovely daughter decides to have a "small" party with fifteen or so kids. Once the party is discovered, and her friends text *their* friends, dozens more teens and young adults show up, who turn the house into what looks like a fraternity party, with spilled beer and wine, broken heirlooms, disgruntled neighbors, and ultimately a visit from the police to break it up.

For the life of you, you can't understand how your daughter could have done such an irresponsible and careless thing! After all, she's generally so *reliable*. In this case, what she did actually required planning and even deception—so she had to have known at least some of the potential consequences of her actions. It was her dopamine-induced tendency to minimize negative consequences in favor of the possibility of fun, stimulation, and status with her peers that prompted this very poor decision.

A third effect of the increased dopamine release is an increased risk of addiction. The drive for pleasure will lead many teens toward drugs and alcohol or other addicting substances and behaviors, such as sugary foods, risky sexual behavior, and pornography. The dopamine-based highs and lows that the addictive substance or behavior creates can seduce teens into the trap of chronic use to find the highs, only to be met shortly after by the lows, driving the desire to achieve the highs again and again.

How Does This Information Help?

So what is the purpose of heightened dopamine activity in teenagers? After all, isn't it a major cause of problems and accidents? Well, yes it is. But it is also the driving force to innovate, search, create, and take the necessary risks and opportunities to discover themselves and the world. This is the essential work of adolescence, and we need to embrace it. As parents we want to support opportunities for our teenagers to explore, challenge, and grow their abilities. This can happen in classrooms, in after-school activities, as well as during home and community activities. We can engage our teenagers in finding their own solutions to the problems they encounter. We can support our teens in finding safe ways for them to express their passions. When we create opportunities for our teenagers to challenge themselves and engage in life, we are helping them to develop their brains so that their understanding of themselves and others grows, and their ability to make coherent, high-quality decisions improves.

The pruning back of neurons has critical implications for our teenagers. When they involve themselves in deep learning and developing specific areas of interest and skill, they will maintain and grow the parts of the brain that facilitate those areas. When they learn a musical instrument, develop foreign language or math skills, play a sport, or rebuild a car engine, our teens are building neurological connections—and abilities—that will last a lifetime. And even if they put these skills away for a while, they'll be there when they go back to them later in life—just like riding a bike.

Remember that the prefrontal cortex in teens is in this important developmental stage, so full neurological integration—the ability to understand their own and others' feelings, make high-quality decisions, and use intuition—is still in process. One way this incomplete development is commonly demonstrated is in teenagers' difficulty when it comes to reading others. They might believe that other kids don't like them when that is not the case at all. They think that a parent is angry with them when the parent is only emphasizing a point. "Why do you always have to yell at me?" they'll say. It's not uncommon to hear a teenager say, "My teacher hates me!"—only to find out from the teacher that she is actually quite fond of the kid and is simply trying to motivate him to try harder.

So what's a parent to do? All this information helps us understand that our teens need both structure and opportunity to grow and develop, but in a safe context. It helps us know that in spite of how our kids are behaving, they aren't necessarily being oppositional or simply choosing to be "bad." Rather, they are adjusting and responding to the many changes they are undergoing, and they need our understanding, support, and structure. So if we can manage to not take all this too personally, and refrain from feeding the Control Battle Beast, we'll be the resource our kids need us to be now, supporting their growth into happy, empowered, and successful young adults.

But the challenges on this journey sometimes get the better of us. Even with the best of intentions, parents and teens can find themselves locked in a control battle, and this can seriously limit all the growing and developing our teens need to do. The next chapter will help you understand more precisely what feeds the Beast, and Part 2 will give you the tools to end it.

CHAPTER 3

What Feeds the Beast?

We've established there is this Beast living in our space. Now it's time to talk about what feeds the Beast. When we figure out what the Beast feeds on, we'll be able to starve it. To do that, we need to examine the elements that provide nourishment to this pattern we're calling the Control Battle.

In a typical control battle, three key nutrients provide the perfect food to sustain the Beast and enable the control battle to thrive: reactivity, overfocusing on the other, and a negative emotional tone.

Reactivity

Reactivity is when we respond to another person automatically without thinking about what we're saying or doing, with a reaction that is more instinctual or impulsive than well thought out. Being reactive is, in many ways, quite natural. We can't always stop and configure a well-reasoned response to the infinite number of things going on around us. If it starts to get dark, we turn on a light—and may not even notice that we did it. We simply do it.

Sometimes our instinctual reactions are perfectly appropriate to a situation. Grabbing a child's arm to pull her from the path of an oncoming car can be a lifesaving reaction. We have so many interactions with our family members from day to day, there is no way we can possibly consider everything we say and every response we make to what someone else says.

How Reactivity Feeds the Beast

Overuse of reactivity, however, can build or maintain a control battle. When we react to what is being said or done without taking charge of our thoughts and actions, we are letting the situation control us. In other words, we are giving away our self-control and instead allowing ourselves to be controlled by the other person's actions. The opposite of reactivity is thoughtful communication or thoughtful action. When we take a moment to think about what is going on, or what is being said, and choose a healthy, thoughtful response, we are in charge of ourselves.

When my behavior is controlled by my teen, and my teen's behavior is controlled by me, neither of us is taking control of ourselves. We are simply reacting to—and, ironically, being controlled by—each other. When this happens, we open the door to the Control Battle.

Contributors to Reactivity

Stress, frustration, fear, and anger all increase the tendency to be reactive and leave little room for thoughtfulness. When we're rested and calm, we're far more able to be sensitive and thoughtful to those around us. Conversely, when we're stressed and tired, the littlest things can bother us. And to make matters worse, the presence of a control battle tends to raise emotions and cause stress, encouraging even more reactivity. This vicious cycle is one way the control battle develops momentum. Two other factors that contribute to reactivity, and hence the control battle, are temperament and personalization.

Temperament

Some people are more emotionally sensitive than others and may tend to react more quickly or intensely. Some may be naturally competitive and inclined to "win" an interaction. Childrearing experts Ron Taffel and Melinda Blau, in their excellent book, *Nurturing Good Children Now* (2000), present an illuminating section on individual temperament and how it affects children and their parents. Taffel and Blau explain that temperament is inherited, which means it's passed on genetically, and is an innate part of personality. We each have a unique temperament, or basic nature, that we experience and carry with us throughout our lives. According to Taffel and Blau, children do best when parented in a way that accepts and works with their basic temperament. In other words, when we try to change children's or teens' basic nature, blame them, or get upset with them for their temperament, it will invariably invite a control battle. This can also help us understand why we may have a control battle with one of our children and not another.

The four basic temperament types. Taffel and Blau describe four basic temperament types: intense/aggressive, intense/sensitive, reserved/clingy, and easy/balanced. Intense/aggressive kids are out in front, creating the action, and they can be very competitive. They lack patience and can become frustrated by obstacles. As young children, they may have been the ones throwing tantrums. These teenagers have lots of initiative and, when inspired, may expect everyone else to go along with their plans. When they engage in a sport or activity, it isn't enough to simply enjoy it, they need to win. And even if they're only competing against themselves, they'll be frustrated if they don't perform the way they wanted to.

Intense/sensitive kids are also very active. What distinguishes this group is their intense reactions to discomforts and slights. These teens are happy to participate and give their very best. But when things don't work out or they get personally rebuffed, they can become very hurt and angry. Don't make the mistake of telling these individuals to "get over it; it's no big deal," because it sure doesn't feel that way to them and their upset feelings will only intensify.

Reserved/clingy kids are sensitive to their environment and don't enjoy large chaotic social settings, generally preferring quiet, more intimate situations. They don't like fierce competition and can easily get their feelings hurt, often retreating when they do. They need a boost of self-confidence as they move into the socially challenging environment of adolescence. Encourage these kids too much, though, and they are likely to feel pushed and resist more. Ignore them, and they'll feel hurt. Meet them where they're at, and things will go smoothly.

Easy/balanced kids are generally easy to raise. They can be happy in a wide variety of situations, and problems and hurts seem to just roll off their backs. These kids can get themselves in plenty of trouble, like any other teenager; it's just that they're a bit more emotionally resilient and have an easier time in relationships.

Working within our teen's basic nature. All four of these temperament types have inherent strengths and weaknesses. But by accepting and working within the reality of their basic nature, we can help our kids bring out their best and minimize their weaknesses. Even if they were comfortable with their basic nature as younger children, teens will need to relearn to accept and manage their temperament in their new adolescent bodies and minds, and in the new social environment of adolescence.

When there is a mismatch in temperament between a parent and teen, there is a greater likelihood of reactivity and risk of entering the control battle. You might easily imagine, for instance, how an intense/aggressive parent might get into a whopper of a control battle with a reserved/clingy child. So understanding our own basic nature, as well as the nature of our teen, will help us curb our tendency to become reactive. We can be more patient with one another, interact more harmoniously, and avoid feeding the Beast.

If you find yourself easily frustrated and you realize you're being reactive with your teenager, ask yourself these questions:

- What is my teenager's basic temperament?

- What is *my* basic temperament?

- Where are we mismatched?

- Where can I be more flexible and accepting of my teenager's temperament?

- What are some ways that I can help my teenager be more aware of—and skilled at—managing his or her temperament?

Despite the important role of temperament, as a therapist who has worked with thousands of individuals, each having their own unique set of characteristics, I've observed that the one characteristic that makes the most difference in social and emotional effectiveness has nothing to do with any specific temperament. It is an individual's level of self-awareness and flexibility. Those adults who have the most self-awareness, including an ability to modify their personal weaknesses and actively utilize their strengths, are the most effective parents, and in general the most effective people. These individuals have the fewest interpersonal conflicts, and they are able to respond most effectively to situations out of their personal comfort zones.

So what we really want for our teens is for them to become aware of their own innate characteristics, to accept themselves, and to manage their strengths and weaknesses in self-valuing and productive ways.

Personalization

Besides temperament, the tendency to engage in what thera-pists call *personalization* can influence reactivity.

The easiest way to understand personalization is to think about what happens when we allow our ego to get hurt by other people's words or actions. Instead of their words or actions affirm-ing us, or making us feel good, they make us feel bad about our-selves. In fact, others' words and actions more accurately reflect on *them*, not us, so personalization is something we should all work to reduce. We're all vulnerable to being hurt by others, but if we're too vulnerable to getting our feelings hurt by our teenager, we'll more easily react and get caught up in a control battle.

When our feelings are at stake, we often spring into action—to *react*—before we think at all. A good example of this happens commonly with stepparents. Let's say a new stepmother extends herself to support and love her husband's children in an attempt to create a bond and help the children feel comfortable with her. After an initial honeymoon period, the children start testing limits and asserting that the stepmother isn't their "real" mother, so they don't have to respect her or acknowledge her authority. Often a stepmother will feel very hurt and angry when kids display this attitude. *After I tried so hard, and was so good to them, how dare they treat me in this way? They're just spoiled brats!* she says to herself—or, worse yet, out loud to the children. In this case she's taking a natural dynamic in a blended family relationship and making it personal.

Here are some examples of personalizing language.

Parents:

You don't respect me.

You're punishing me for divorcing your father!

Why don't you ever listen to me?

Do you know how hard I have to work for you to waste things?

Why are you doing this to me?

Kids:

Why do you criticize everything I do?

You hate my friends!

You don't care about my feelings!

You never want me to have any fun!

You just like taking things away from me!

You love my sister more than me.

The lost opportunities of personalizing. When we personalize what the other person is saying, several things happen. Instead of hearing the other's thoughts and feelings, we hear only our own thoughts and feelings about what that person is saying. Usually, the other's words and tone feel hurtful in some way, and that is what we are actually reacting to. When we understand and change this tendency, we begin to starve the Beast.

Richey

Richey's father asked his son to help him clean up the garage. The mess in the garage is mostly a result of Richey using his father's tools to work on his motorcycle, so Richey's father thinks he's being pretty nice to offer his son the opportunity to clean the garage together, instead of making him to do it alone. He's even thinking it might be a good way to connect with his son. But to his surprise and chagrin, Richey tells him he's too busy to clean the garage.

Richey's father is instantly livid. "What do you mean, you're *too busy?*" he erupts. "You think you can just make

37

messes like that and have everyone else clean up after you?" Clearly Richey's father is responding to his own feelings about Richey's response, with no real understanding of what is going on with Richey. Richey's father is feeling rejected and unappreciated. He is personalizing his son's words and behavior.

When we personalize, we miss a lot of what is truly going on. Rather than understanding what's taking place around us, we pay attention only to our feelings about what is happening. *Does this affirm me or does it hurt me? Does it make me feel good, or does it make me feel bad? Does this mean that I'll get what I want, or does it mean I won't?*

Richey's father might have said to himself, *I wonder if Richey is busy with something important right now.* He could have connected with Richey to find out. He might have learned that Richey has a legitimately busy day and determined they should plan the garage cleanup for the next day. Or he might have learned that Richey's plans *were* flexible, and that the garage cleanup can rightfully come first. In either case, the connection might have been a positive one, and Richey's dad could have learned a little more about Richey.

Whose movie are we watching? In any relationship between two people, there are always two "movies" playing at the same time. One movie reflects reality as *we* experience it, and the other movie reflects the reality of the other person. The question is, which movie are we going to watch—our own movie, or the other person's?

A technique I like to teach my clients is how to consciously allow one of the movies to move into the foreground while letting the other one recede. When we are focusing on what is going on with the other person (watching his or her movie), we are aware of our own internal responses, but we keep them in the background. Then, when we focus on our own reality, we stay mindful that the other person's reality is very different from ours, and that it is still running in the background.

When we personalize, not only do we lose the opportunity to understand more about our teenagers' feelings and activities, we also miss the chance to learn about their thinking, and to assess their level of maturity. When we stay away from personalizing and reacting, we create an opportunity for the other person to feel listened to, understood, validated, and supported, and we allow a deeper conversation to develop. We're better able to help our teens think through their choices, and maybe even learn from us. On the other hand, when we personalize and react, invariably our kids will in turn personalize our responses, feel like they're our victims, and learn nothing from the situation.

What if Richey had told his father that the reason he was too busy to help with the garage was that he'd promised his baseball coach he would compile some critical team statistics for the afternoon's practice? Richey's dad could be reassured that Richey was being a responsible kid. If Richey had told his father—while lying on his bed reading a motorcycle magazine—that he was too busy because his mom told him he had to clean his room, Richey's dad might assess the situation and decide that his son was putting off both responsibilities and needed some parental coaching to help manage his responsibilities.

In order to effectively learn about, assess, coach, and support our kids, we must be willing to watch *their* movie at times, not just our own. When we let our thoughts and feelings become distinct from theirs, we won't be so prone to personalize. And if we don't personalize, we won't be so inclined to react.

Overfocusing on the Other Person

A second element of the control battle involves *overfocusing on the other* person's behavior instead of focusing on ourselves and our own behavior.

We can't change the behavior of another. This is a critical point—and one that is widely misunderstood. Virtually every family that comes into counseling with me is struggling with their child or teenager's behavior and looking for ways to change it. But here's the deal: no one can really change another person's behavior. We can only choose ways to *respond* to another's behavior.

For parents, the truth of this usually manifests when we make it our objective to get our teens to do something we think they should be doing. This may sound normal to you—even appropriate, but think about it: if a teen is dead set against doing something, it may require sheer force to get him to do it—if you can do so at all! And of course the use of force or violence is a horrible idea for many reasons.

One of my adult clients told me that when he was a small boy, his father had been so intent on getting him to eat his peas at dinner one night that he wrestled him to the floor and forced the peas down his throat. I don't remember who won that particular struggle, but I would guess (and hope!) most parents would be unwilling to go that far to get their children to obey them. Even if an act of force was successful in getting a child to consume his peas, I can guarantee you that it had another less desirable effect: it fed and strengthened the control battle.

We are far better off understanding that our teenagers are in charge of their behavior and that as parents we are in charge of ours. It is our kid's job to manage the business of being a kid, and our job to manage the business of being parents. The roles are very different, and when we overfocus on the other person's role and behavior, and what about it that we don't like, we are much more likely to react to it in a misguided effort to change it.

You are not responsible for your teen's behavior!

If you think about it, this can be a very liberating idea: *You are not responsible for your teen's behavior.* Your teenager is responsible for his or her own behavior—not you. You are only responsible for how you *respond* to it. Trying to change your teen not only supports the control battle; it can also lead to your own parental burnout.

If it was really our job to change something we didn't have direct control over, we would naturally feel extremely frustrated, helpless, hopeless, and ultimately exhausted and depressed. Not to mention the burden that would place on our kids. We must always convey the message to our children and teens that they are responsible for their behavior. That way, *they* get the credit when they act responsibly, and *they* are held accountable when they don't.

I'm not saying parents should "do nothing" in response to their children's behavior. While our kids are responsible for their own behavior, we as adults need to be responsible for ours. That means being active in our role as parents. But the minute we try to directly control a teenager's behavior, the teen will resist us, and a control battle will begin—or continue growing.

Let's take a closer look at the parental role. Parental functions include nurturing, setting limits, providing support, and offering guidance or coaching. Confusion and the potential for over-focusing on the other often occurs around setting limits. A parent may ask, "So what's the difference between holding my son accountable for doing his homework and trying to get him to do his homework?"

"Great question!" I'll respond. "Because the difference is critical. Only your kids can get themselves to do their homework. You can't force them to do their homework any more effectively than you can force them to eat their peas. What you *can* do is monitor the doing of the homework, assign a time that homework must be done, observe the quality with which it is being done, provide resources and support, and establish the privileges that are contingent upon doing the homework."

Saying, "You get upstairs and clean your room right now, young man, or you'll be grounded for the whole day!" will be a lot less effective than saying, "Remember, your room needs to be cleaned before I drive you downtown this afternoon." This can lead to your kid having the thought, *Well, I think I'll clean my room so that I can go out.*

In chapter 5, I'll show you how you can hold your teens accountable and put the responsibility for their behavior squarely in their court.

So what does this concept of overfocusing on the other look like from a teen's point of view? When kids overfocus on their parents' behavior, rather than on their own, they become active participants in the control battle. For instance, a teenage girl might think, "Why do my parents care so much about my room being clean? It's *my* room. I should be able to keep it anyway I want! I'll just stuff my things in the closet and that will get them off my back." By looking at her parents' behavior instead of her own, she will stay mired in a control battle, and she won't learn how to organize or keep her things clean. Her energy remains focused on managing her parents (getting them off her back) instead of managing herself and cleaning her room.

A Negative Emotional Tone

Using *a negative emotional tone* when communicating with your teenager is the third element that supports the parent-teen control battle. When we hear a negative tone in the voice of someone talking to us, we automatically assume that person is against us, or presents a threat. And like other mammals, we are programmed to react instinctively to any perceived threat with a fight-or-flight response. As soon as we determine that someone is upset with us, we have a physiological response that prepares us to run away or get ready for conflict. This instinct often encourages us to react in ways that will drive a control battle. So it's crucial, when attempting to reverse a control battle, that we stay positive in our tone. We can see how this works in reverse. When our kids use a positive and respectful tone with us, it's a lot easier for us to listen and offer them the benefit of the doubt.

When you're trying to get free of the control battle, a negative emotional tone definitely sends the wrong message. Instead, send a positive, affirming message that is reflective of your true, broader intentions, which is to help your teen grow up happy and successful. When we need to be stern, we want our tone to be perceived as serious, not threatening.

Your words can project a positive tone. For example, "I know you love your phone and we want you to enjoy it. In order to keep it, you need to put it away at dinnertime without the big struggle we've been having."

Or, "I know you're upset that you can't go out tonight. You should know that I'm on your side, and I'd love for you to be able to go out and do fun things when the opportunity comes. In order for me to allow that, I need to see that you are fully committed to managing your responsibilities."

If we communicate with unbridled anger, the message is most likely to be interpreted as, *My parents are against me.* If our teens reach that conclusion, it can easily start or help maintain a control battle: *If my mom is against me, I've got to defend myself against her.* Instead of listening, learning, and growing, the adolescent fights and resists.

The Sound of a Negative Emotional Tone

So what does a negative tone sound like? Generally speaking, a negative tone is loud and commanding:

I TOLD YOU TO PUT OUT THE GARBAGE!

STOP FIGHTING WITH YOUR SISTER!

GET UPSTAIRS AND CLEAN YOUR ROOM RIGHT NOW!

I TOLD YOU NOT TO EAT IN THE LIVING ROOM. NOW LOOK WHAT YOU DID!

But a negative tone can also be quiet and tense, communicated through clenched teeth. Even the silent treatment can be experienced as hostility or "trying to make me feel guilty."

Along with a negative tone, parents may ask a question that's really an angry statement:

WHY DID YOU DO THAT?

WHAT'S THE MATTER WITH YOU?

HOW MANY TIMES DO I NEED TO TELL YOU TO GET OFF THE COMPUTER?

WHAT DO YOU THINK YOU'RE DOING?

WHO DO YOU THINK YOU ARE?

DO YOU HAVE TO SCREW THINGS UP EVERY TIME I TRUST YOU?

There is no reasonable way for teenagers to respond to this. So they just experience the hostility, and they yell right back; or they stuff it inside and store it up for the next round.

The Sound of a Positive Emotional Tone

And what does a positive tone sound like? In general, a positive tone is warmer, softer, and more soothing than what you just read. It's expressed best when you stay in touch with the caring and love you have for your teenager. That way your tone will be authentic and will invite the best response. A positive tone arises naturally when we think of communication as something that is intended to deliver an important message, not just change a behavior or get one's feelings out in the open. And when it needs to be firm, the emphasis is on the behavior rather than on the person committing the behavior.

"I know I already asked you to take the garbage out, Sean, but I'd like you to do it now, please. It's overflowing and I want to get the kitchen finished up before I sit down."

"I need the fighting to stop *now*, please. Either talk to each other respectfully or take a break, but I need a quieter house."

"I see you're having trouble getting off the computer, but I need you to come to dinner now, please."

"I'm surprised you did that. I think of you as more thoughtful than that."

"I understand that you're angry with me, but you're going to need to be a lot more respectful when you talk to me."

"I'm sorry that you didn't use this opportunity to build trust with us. What went wrong?"

"I'm on your side."

Remember, inside your teen is a great kid. Let's assume that your teen is simply caught up in the control battle, and otherwise is a terrific young person who needs your support, guidance, and mentoring.

Here's a technique that can help. Talk to the part of your teen who is wonderful, the person you know your teen can be.

In control battle–based relationships with our teens, it is easy to feel we are on opposite sides. We may find we are acting against each other as opponents, or even enemies. To have any hope of successfully exiting a control battle, it is vital that we remember to communicate in the words and tone that convey the message, *I'm on your side.*

So if we can begin to eliminate the three nutrients the Control Battle Beast requires—reactivity, overfocusing on the other, and a negative emotional tone—we can begin to starve the Beast, align with our teens, and make it clear that we're on their side.

PART TWO

STARVING THE BEAST

CHAPTER 4

A Healthy Vision

In the next three chapters we'll talk about the essential steps required to move out of a control battle–based relationship, and I'll show you how to shift responsibility and accountability to your teen. But any attempt to accomplish this will come up short unless you can learn to hold a healthy vision of your teenager, and to communicate this vision to him or her. Holding a healthy vision of your teen can help you reestablish your moral authority and leadership while starving the Beast. Let's see how this works.

What Is a Healthy Vision?

In order to move forward successfully with any venture in life, we must hold a vision of a successful outcome. This is true of athletics, business, or personal ventures of any kind. Success takes more than a vision; it takes knowledge, skill, resources, and hard work. But without a vision of success, problems and obstacles will be discouraging, overwhelming, and defeating. Lack of vision may even cause a person to give up.

This simple truth applies to parenting as well. When we first think of becoming parents, we imagine ourselves having lovable children who will grow up to be happy and successful. We have a healthy and positive vision of them and who they will grow to become.

When we do become parents, our children reveal who they are and their potential for the future in small increments, gradually, like flower buds with promise. A flower bud is beautiful in every stage, yet at each stage we anticipate its full flower. So it is with children. "Robert is very clever. Perhaps he will invent things!" "Rosa is so dramatic. She could excel on stage." "Randy is strong like Grandpa. He will be a star on the football field." "Suzanne loves reading and learning. I can see her as a college professor."

Even when we have a healthy vision of our children, we know and expect there will be challenges along the way—and we are rarely disappointed in this regard! But we don't want to let go of our healthy vision of who they are and will become. This positive vision gives us a perspective from which to accept and address problems as they arise. We don't panic or lose faith in our children when something goes awry. We see problems within a context that is essentially positive.

A healthy vision gives us a sense of direction, and when we know where we're going, we are more likely to take problems in stride. When you're hiking in the mountains and you get hungry, thirsty, and exhausted, if you know how long the hike is going to be, and you have faith in your map and your ability to negotiate the terrain, you're likely to accept the discomfort as part of the hike and you'll enjoy the trees, the views, and the experience in general. But on the exact same hike, if you're unsure of where you are or where you're going, you might feel a sense of panic. You're certainly not enjoying the hike, the trees, or the views if you're worried about being lost and possibly dying of exposure.

How Do We Lose Our Way?

When problems with our teenagers start to emerge and their new adolescent behaviors catch us off guard, we can lose faith in our "map"—our sense of where things are going. And that can lead to panic and a loss of faith in our teenager. When this happens, it's very easy for parents to become reactive, to overfocus on changing the teen's behavior, and to use a very negative tone, a tone that represents their panic. As we learned from the previous chapter, that's a recipe for fattening the Beast. And just as losing faith in our teens can help nourish control battles, control battles can cause us to lose faith in our teens. They can destroy the healthy and positive vision we hold of them and their future.

The Making of a Negative Vision

Let's say your teenager has been exhibiting disrespectful behavior at home. The resulting pattern of arguing and fighting is starting to look like a control battle. You may be personalizing your teenager's behavior, feeling pretty darned frustrated, angry, and maybe even a little hurt. When we start to carry all those negative feelings, it becomes hard to carry positive thoughts as well. Positive thoughts and negative feelings don't fit together easily in the same mind. It's hard to feel frustrated, hurt, and angry, and still be thinking what a wonderful teenager you have.

So when our feelings dwell in the negative, we will eventually change our thoughts to match our feelings. Healthy positive thoughts will sooner or later give way to negative thoughts that match our negative feelings. These negative thoughts and feelings will create a negative vision. "Robert can't follow simple instructions. He has to do everything his own way." "Rosa is so attention-seeking. She has to be the center of every group." "Randy is too competitive. Why does he have to win all the time?"

Let's see how the loss of a positive vision affected a girl named Sonya and her parents.

Sonya

Sonya was a bright and capable sixteen-year-old who came to me for counseling. She had an older brother who was

51

academically gifted and was attending college as a biology major. Like her brother, Sonya was bright, and she was an accomplished musician as well. However, she was less independent than her brother and required significantly more structure and support.

Sonya did extremely well in elementary school, which provided the structure and support she needed to thrive. When she hit adolescence and entered middle school, her school performance declined dramatically and she gravitated toward friendships with other kids who were doing poorly. Sonya's parents had the expectation that Sonya would simply proceed through her adolescence much as her brother had: independently and with a strong sense of purpose. When that didn't happen, her parents became upset with her, and Sonya reacted by avoiding them and tuning them out.

And so a control battle emerged that completely dominated their relationship. This control battle interfered with her parents' ability to evaluate Sonya's situation objectively and make healthy decisions together. As a result, Sonya did not receive the structure and support she needed and was seriously underfunctioning. She had left high school and was attending an independent study program where she was barely challenged. She often smoked marijuana and spent most of her time hanging out with friends. The one positive area of her life was the community-based musical group she played with.

In addition to this loss of opportunity for academic, social, and emotional development for Sonya, the control battle had given Sonya's parents a profoundly negative view of her. They saw her as a failure on the road to disaster, and overlooked her strengths. While she was indeed very argumentative, she was also very engaging, with excellent verbal skills. She was quite insightful about people and showed keen awareness of human nature. But sadly, these strengths went unnoticed by her parents.

"Sonya is lazy and unmotivated," said her mother. "It's too late to do anything about it. If I try to push her, we just get into fights. She thinks everything I expect of her is annoying and when I ask her to do something, it will be done only halfway if it's done at all. So I've given up asking anything of her. She spends all her time hanging out with her friends and does maybe three hours of schoolwork a week. She expects me to pay for everything she needs, and if I try to set up some conditions, it turns into a fight. When we refuse to give her what she wants, she badgers us relentlessly. How will she be able to manage in life? We can't take care of her forever!"

Sonya's parents did assume some responsibility for the problem. "We didn't ask enough of her before," they admit. "And now it's too late." But even though they acknowledged their own part in the scenario, they maintained a negative vision of their daughter. They viewed Sonya as spoiled, unmotivated, and undisciplined: a lost cause.

Sonya had a negative view of things as well. She saw her parents as having little insight into who she really was as a person and felt they focused only on the negatives. She didn't feel close to either her mother or her father, and although she sometimes longed for that closeness, she feared it, not trusting it could ever exist—and so she simply avoided them.

With a severe control battle defining their relationship, both Sonya and her parents felt increasingly hopeless, and their vision of each other and the relationship became increasingly negative. This negative vision is a significant element that supported the control battle.

Sadly, this situation did not turn around, and I imagine that Sonya did not have a smooth transition into young adulthood. This particular family was extremely entrenched and unable to change directions.

Fortunately, most families I see are far more flexible and responsive. In the counseling room, before we ever begin to talk about problems, we focus on and highlight all of a teen's strengths and the family's strengths as well. Once we have a healthy vision clearly in front of us, we have a promising context within which we can understand and solve problems, and end the control battle.

In order for Sonya's parents to have ended the control battle, they needed to cultivate a healthy view of their daughter. A realistic and healthy perspective can be expressed in many ways: "Sonya is clearly not realizing her potential, and we need to address this with her. We need her to get back on the right track and start making progress. I'm sure with our help and support she can be very successful. Sonya is a smart, talented, and engaging young woman. In spite of all her problems, she has some great things going for her. We can emphasize this with her and introduce appropriate and important expectations. She needs and deserves our support right now, even if she doesn't act that way."

Positive Visions Are Not Always Healthy

Having a positive vision, however, may not necessarily be healthy if the vision is unrealistic, uninformed, or rigid. Such visions can backfire, resulting in exactly what you are hoping to avoid: an unhealthy outcome for your teen, or a damaging control battle.

Denial Is Not a Healthy Vision

Some parents are inclined to be overly optimistic and may overlook serious problems. If Sonya's parents had taken this approach, it might have sounded like this: "Sonya is just going through a rebellious period. Of course she doesn't want to listen to her parents. I didn't either when I was her age! High school isn't for everyone. She can always go back to school when she knows what she wants to do. I was a late bloomer too. So she just wants to hang out with her friends, well, that's normal. And aren't all teenagers smoking a little weed these days? After all, it's not like she's getting arrested or anything."

This false front, pretending "everything is just fine," would not address Sonya's need for structure and support, and would only encourage the status quo. Sonya would be less likely to develop her character or her abilities to their full potential, and worse, she might continue on a path of drug use and other self-destructive behaviors.

A Rigid Vision Is Not a Healthy Vision

Another way that a vision can be "positive" yet unhealthy is when parents have a fixed view of who their child is and needs to become. Seeing potential in some area, parents can push beyond what is realistic or healthy.

I'm reminded of Steven, whose son Jeff was an extraordinarily talented baseball player.

Jeff

Jeff's athletic talent and interests stretched into a variety of sports and activities. However, his father became enraged when Jeff showed interest in pursuing any sport or activity other than baseball. "Can't you see what you're throwing away?" Steven would exclaim in frustration. Initially, Jeff complied with his father's demands and devoted himself to baseball. He went to all the baseball camps and entered all the competitions his father required him to. As he got older, however, Jeff defied his father, and a control battle of epic proportion grew. Jeff eventually quit baseball altogether and became an avid snowboarding competitor. His father refused to attend any of Jeff's snowboarding competitions, and they eventually stopped speaking to each other.

How Do We Create a Healthy Vision of Our Teen?

Creating a healthy vision of our teenagers requires two things. One is having the faith that they will grow up to be excellent adults—that they have what they need to grow, and will continue to grow throughout their lives. The second part of a healthy vision is the ability to see the process of growing up as a rich and enjoyable journey. And that means holding a healthy vision of our kids throughout their teenage years.

Remember our hike through the mountains? With a good map and confidence that you know where you're going, you're able to enjoy the hike. You don't know exactly what each part of the hike is going to be like, and that's a big part of what makes it enjoyable. Having faith in the outcome gives you the peace of mind to endure the challenges and enjoy the rewards along the way.

Once we're confident that our teenager will grow to be a healthy, self-reliant adult, we're free to have a healthy vision of the journey and enjoy its rewards.

Here are some ways to establish and hold a healthy vision of your teenager.

- Understand and accept your teen's basic temperament. All temperaments have inherent strengths as well as challenges. It's easy to be aware of the challenges and see them as liabilities, but remember to tune in to your teen's strengths and appreciate them. Also, understand that as they go through life, your kids will learn ways to address the challenges that their inherent temperaments present. You don't have to "fix" them before they turn eighteen years old.

- Beyond his or her temperament, your teenager has many skills, talents, and attributes; makes healthy choices; and engages in fulfilling activities. Be sure you are aware of and appreciate these things.

- A healthy vision needs to be expressed. By communicating what you enjoy and appreciate about your teenager, it reinforces that healthy vision and allows your teen to see him- or herself through your confident eyes. Don't be shy to ask about your teen's experiences, feelings, and thoughts. When you do, and are impressed with the responses you get, your teen will feel seen and approved of. You don't have to fix or change his or her point of view, simply appreciate it. In this way you are giving your "vote of confidence." You are sending the message that you have a healthy vision of your teen.

- Remember to support and acknowledge your teen in failure as well as in success. Life isn't about A's or wins. Life is about growing and learning, and if we're afraid to fail, we won't take the necessary risks to succeed.

A Healthy Vision of Yourself

And finally, it's important to have a healthy vision of yourself. When our kids start heading over that adolescent footbridge, they sure don't spend a lot of time appreciating us or trying to make us feel good. I've never heard a kid say, "Wow, Dad! That was a fabulous limit you set with me." And I'm willing to bet you haven't heard words to that effect either. So you've got to take it on faith that your best effort is excellent, even if you aren't at your best 24/7.

Our teenagers need us and appreciate us more than we know, and more than they can easily express. Even if our teens do manage to convey gratitude, their eyes are moving forward and their job is independence, so making us feel good about our parenting is not high on their list.

In spite of the fact that you feel pushed away, are told you "don't get it," or somehow feel inadequate, don't believe it. Have a positive vision of your teenager, a positive vision of yourself, and a positive vision of this journey—and your best efforts will take you far.

CHAPTER 5

The Power of Earned Privileges

B y harnessing the power of earned privileges, parents can put an end to the stress and futility of trying to change their teen's behavior and put that responsibility back where it belongs, squarely in the hands of their teenager. And when teenagers are in charge of their behavior, it's amazing how well they can do.

Let's take a closer look at this critical concept.

In family life where kids are essentially responsible and respect-ful, when a kid breaks a rule or doesn't manage a responsibility, the parents will give a "consequence" for the behavior, such as taking something away. This serves the purpose of communicating that a behavior won't be tolerated; the kid gets the message and behaves differently to avoid getting that consequence again. The conse-quence could be something like being grounded for a weekend, having restricted driving privileges for two weeks, or losing a cell phone for a couple of days. This loss gets the message across, and the behavior improves.

In a control battle–based relationship, however, giving conse-quences will be maddeningly ineffective. It may change a behavior for a brief period of time, but the problem will soon return in one form or another. A teen may be contrite and say it won't happen again, but it does. Or, the teen may be defiant, invite the consequence, and have an I-don't-care attitude. "Go ahead, ground me forever. I hate my life anyway." Or have you heard this one? "That's so stupid. Grounding me isn't going to help. It's just going to make me madder and then I really won't do what you want." In fact, when there is a parent-teen control battle operating, giving a consequence and taking something away from the teen will actually drive the existing control battle.

So in order to effectively end the Control Battle and starve the Beast, we must examine the characteristics of consequences versus privileges and shift explicitly to the concept of earned privileges. This will allow you to reestablish both accountability and appropriately high standards for your teen.

Why Earned Privileges Matter

Let's examine the subtle yet profound distinction between giving a consequence for a transgression and withholding a privilege. When we impose a consequence, it can be interpreted that the activity or item being lost belongs to the teen, and we as parents are taking it away as punishment for wrongdoing. The control battle–involved teen will consider that the parent is "doing something to me: taking away my freedom, not allowing me to use my phone, not letting me watch TV." These teens can experience themselves as victims of their unreasonable parents who are "coming down on them." They will not get the message that they *need to take responsibility and change a behavior,* and instead the consequence will only drive the control battle.

The word "privilege," on the other hand, implies that the object or activity in question is of high value and should not be taken for granted. Privileges come along with accomplishments. They are earned. They are not entitlements. Losing or gaining the object or activity is the responsibility of the teenager.

What parents want is a change in attitude and behavior. They want their kids to learn and grow. Establishing that privileges are *earned* allows parents to empower their teens to learn and grow throughout their adolescence.

Privileges are based on an essential trust between the teen and parent: trust that the given object or activity will be managed in positive ways. For instance, the privilege to go out with friends on Friday night is based on trust that the teen will come home on time. The privilege to have a cell phone includes the expectation that parental texts and calls will be answered. The privilege to use a car is premised on it being driven safely and legally, and returned in good condition. A lost privilege communicates to the teen that the implied trust has been broken; the conditions of the privilege are not being met, and it will require effort to repair the trust and reestablish the conditions of the privilege. When the parent is satisfied that the necessary learning has taken place and the teen's attitude and behavior is healthy, the desired privileges can then be reinstated.

Because they want their kids to be happy, loving and support-ive parents *will* give their kids all kinds of things simply because their kids want them. This often creates an attitude of entitlement. Teens learn that they'll simply be handed whatever they desire—the keys to the car, TVs in their rooms, cell phones, the opportu-nity to choose how they spend their time, and more.

Many teens will compare themselves to peers who are doing more poorly than they are as justification for why they should be showered with privileges and material objects. "It's not like I'm stealing stuff or getting arrested," they may say. "And I'm passing all my classes." I recently heard a teenager say, "These are the best years of my life. I'm supposed to be having fun!" They have the notion that they are entitled to anything they want, when they want it.

There is nothing in any parenting handbook or any law that says a child is entitled to watch TV; eat out; have dessert; or have a cell phone, computer, or video games; nothing that says the child has the right to go to the movies or to use a car. All these things are privileges, and like all privileges, must be earned.

It is absolutely critical that we as parents establish a relationship between what kids are given and how they perform. It's best to teach this concept when our children are young. Yet in many cases we'll still have to reestablish this essential concept in adolescence.

Exactly what should we consider privileges? Almost everything we give our kids—beyond love and the basics for survival—should be considered privileges that must be earned.

This can include

computers and internet access, except when being used for schoolwork;

access to TV or any electronic entertainment;

cell phones;

skateboards, bikes, surfboards, and use of cars; and

permission to go out to socialize.

In general, when kids are involved in formal activities that include other people, such as a team sport, school play, or even a teen rock band rehearsal prior to a performance, we should not withhold their involvement. We would generally not withdraw privileges such as reading books, drawing or doing art, playing a musical instrument, or doing anything obviously productive.

Let's say your teenage son is not managing schoolwork or home responsibilities, is constantly on his smartphone and computer, and is not getting any physical exercise. You might leave going to the gym and riding a bike as intact privileges but withdraw everything else.

A blended family I was working with had five kids who the parents could not get to cooperate. They said it was constant bedlam and that trying to get things under control was like "herding cats." The parents couldn't think of what privileges they could make conditional on cooperation. When I asked them to describe what the kids did the night before, they reported that they sent out for pizza and the kids watched movies. I didn't even need to respond to this. They had their "ah ha" moment.

Earned Privileges Empower Teens

When it is made clear to them that the privileges they receive are earned, *teens are empowered to take charge of their own destiny.* By managing their responsibilities and forming a relationship with their parents that acknowledges accountability, they are able to establish themselves as trustworthy, and with this comes the knowledge that they can earn virtually anything deemed appropriate.

When teens (and kids of all ages) *earn* privileges, they are far more likely to appreciate and safeguard them. More importantly, they will feel the self-respect that comes from accomplishment, a critical component of happiness. And by establishing the relationship between the privileges they receive and how they perform, we are teaching our teens responsibility and accountability, two very critical social-emotional skills they need for life.

Responsibility and Accountability, the Road to Independence

Here is a basic formula that you and your teenager need to know, either implicitly or explicitly:

Responsibility + Accountability = Trust

Trust + Age = Privileges

Mastering responsibility and accountability can be thought of as an adolescent's road to independence. If our kids are essentially responsible in school, at home, and with their social behavior, we will see this and be inclined to trust them with a broad range of privileges. If they are not responsible, we will see that as well, and will not be inclined to bestow privileges.

If your teen has not yet read the online chapter "For Teens Only," I encourage you to ask him or her to do so. What I explain to kids in that chapter is that virtually everything they say and do, or don't say and don't do, is noticed by their parents and gets logged as either positive and mature, or negative and immature. I ask them to picture a dial on their parent's forehead where the hand of the dial goes counterclockwise when they exhibit irresponsibility or a bad attitude, and clockwise when they exhibit mature, responsible behavior and a positive attitude. I call it the parental mature-o-meter. When kids keep the dial on the right, they get maximum privileges, and when it moves left, they lose them. So if they like to hear the word YES when they ask for a privilege, they need to keep the dial on the right.

Accountability is the way we teach responsibility to our youth. In order for us to grant appropriate privileges to our kids, we must be in charge of the privileges they do and don't receive. This means they are responsible *to the parent* for their actions, and it is the parent who will determine if a privilege has or has not been earned. When we talk with our teens about "accountability," it can often lead to an argument. It's much easier and more understandable to teens if we simply refer to what we're looking for as "a positive attitude." They get that and it works just fine, but it's important for parents to know that we're dealing with the issue of teen accountability to parental authority.

When Do We Grant or Withdraw a Privilege?

We may have excellent reasons for not granting a privilege to our kids. Maybe we see it as unsafe, age or otherwise inappropriate, unhealthy, unaffordable, or perhaps simply not yet earned. We as parents need to honor our own judgment about that. If your teen has earned the privilege in the past, it does not guarantee the right to it in the future. Receiving it again is contingent upon you continuing to see the object or activity as viable, appropriate, and well earned.

If you see a privilege as safe, appropriate, healthy, and affordable, then the question is whether or not you see your teenager as having the ability to manage it. Does she have the sense of responsibility that helps you trust that it will turn out well? Going downtown to meet friends might be appropriate and safe for a fifteen-year-old who is responsible and avoids trouble. If she is current with her responsibilities and has a healthy attitude that enables you to trust her, then it would be a privilege you may grant.

Let's say your daughter is generally allowed to meet her friends downtown after school. But lately you've noticed a change in her attitude and responsibility. Hanging out downtown has become the priority, and her schoolwork has fallen off. When asked about it, she becomes evasive and annoyed with the questioning. At this point, going downtown and hanging out with her friends is no longer appropriate and is not an earned privilege.

Let's look at another example. Jason is a fifteen-year-old who loves action and has a nose for finding and joining trouble. He has a history of evasiveness and lying. Jason is not a good candidate for the privilege of meeting his friends downtown. This, however, is not a permanent condition. Jason can earn this privilege by becoming more responsible and trustworthy.

A common question from parents is, "Do I have to take my kids' privileges away every time they do something wrong?" The answer is absolutely not! We all make mistakes and don't always perform at our best. Remember, we are on their side and want them to be happy and successful. We simply need to know that they are on a learning curve for the growing they need to do. If they make a mistake in judgment with regard to their responsibilities, we can correct them, and they can take responsibility for the error, resolve the issue, and move on.

Juna

Juna is required to do her chores before going out on Saturdays. This has been established and, generally speaking, goes well. Today, however, after Juna has left, her father notices that the chores were done poorly or not at all. When Juna comes home, her father greets her and raises his concerns.

Dad: Juna, what happened with your chores today? Your room isn't picked up, the vacuuming isn't done, and while it looks like the bathroom was gone over, it is far from clean.

Juna: Okay, I'll do it now.

Dad: Thanks, but I'd like to understand what happened. You know the expectation and you usually manage it so well. What happened today?

Juna: Well, I slept in till ten, and I was supposed to meet everyone at eleven. I knew they'd be going off and I wouldn't be able to catch up with them. I was going to do it better when I got back.

Dad: I understand. I expect you to ask first, though, if you're going to change the arrangements.

Juna: So what should I do if you and Mom are out, like you were this morning? I would have missed my friends.

Dad: That's a good question. If you are going to make your own judgment call and you believe it's a situation where we would say yes, leave us a note and call in or text us when you get a chance.

Juna: Sure, okay.

In this case, Juna's dad is pretty confident that Juna understands how to handle the situation and will follow the protocol. Unless things were to continue poorly, he saw no reason to withdraw a privilege. In his communication with Juna, he holds her accountable for her responsibilities, tying them in to her quest for independence. He does this in a respectful manner. And you might be surprised by how reasonable a kid can be when treated with respect while held to accountability.

Let's look at the situation with Juna again. If responsibility had been the only issue and Juna was *not* accountable, the conversation would have gone very differently.

Dad: Juna, what happened with your chores today? Your room isn't picked up, the vacuuming isn't done and, while it looks like the bathroom was gone over, it is far from clean.

Juna: I'm going to do it later.

Dad: I'm glad you're thinking about it, but I'd like to understand what happened. You know the rule; the chores get done before you go out, and you've always been good about it. What happened today?

Juna: What's the difference, as long as it gets done? I take care of my responsibilities.

Dad: Your mom and I want the house picked up before the weekend gets going so that we can enjoy the rest of the weekend.

Juna: That's what you and Mom want, but I do things differently.

Sound familiar?

Many parents will be swayed by this argument. They will see the merit in what Juna is saying, and in fact, she does have a good point; if she manages her responsibilities, perhaps she should be able to decide when and how she does them.

That's simply not how life works, however! In school, the teacher decides when the assignment is due—not the student. At work, whether or not we agree with our bosses, we need to meet their requirements. Accountability to authority is a critical life skill.

Even though Juna may have a reasonable argument, it must be negotiated within a context of accountability. What does that mean? Well, it means that the teenager exhibits a positive attitude, an attitude of *respect* toward the person to whom she is accountable, and accepts that person's decision whether or not she agrees with it.

Losing a Specific Privilege or All Privileges

When a teen is in a control battle with a parent, there is a lack of accountability to the parent, and sometimes it will require a dramatic loss of all privileges to get the teen's attention and push "restart." Otherwise, losing one privilege and then another can feel very much like an escalating war. Let's think about it: a cell phone, recreational use of the Internet, video games, going out with friends, use of a car, and access to pocket money are all privileges that are reasonably granted when teens are managing their primary responsibilities and being respectful and accountable to their parents. So if there is a major breach in the areas of responsibility and accountability, none of those privileges are appropriate and all of them should be revoked.

If, on the other hand, a teen is not managing a responsibility that goes along with a specific privilege, but is otherwise responsible and accountable, then only that specific privilege should be rescinded. In the earlier example, Juna might lose the privilege of going downtown after school. However, if she became oppositional and decided to sneak downtown, or displayed a negative attitude and her schoolwork continued to decline, then a total loss of privileges would become necessary.

When Carlos borrows the car, he returns it dirty, cluttered with fast food bags filled with leftovers. After talking with Carlos, his parents have noticed the behavior hasn't changed much. Yet Carlos is doing well in school, is playing sports, is always home on time, and is finishing his college applications. It's pretty simple: no more car use for Carlos. And how might Carlos regain the privilege of using the car? He can apologize and acknowledge the value of taking care of things, returning borrowed possessions in excellent condition, and showing gratitude for the things he receives. Also, he can detail the car as a way of making amends, demonstrating a commitment to those values and thus reearning the privilege of using the car.

The Magic of the Gap: Reinstating a Lost Privilege

Reinstating a privilege presents the critical opportunity to shift responsibility for changing your teen's behavior from you to your teen. After all—and I'm sorry for being redundant here, but this is huge—who can change your teen's behavior?

It's not you.

It's your teen, and only your teen.

So when your daughter asks, "When will I get my cell phone back?" The answer should be, "I have no idea, Sweetheart. You earned that phone by being responsible and having a good attitude. You lost it for not being responsible and having a lousy attitude. When you earn it again, you'll get it again. I have no control over that, only you do. It's up to you."

It's up to you. When you offer this answer to the question, "When will I get my privileges back?" suddenly a gap is created that allows your teenager to face an unfamiliar juncture and figure out how to respond. And the solution is taking responsibility.

This approach is in stark contrast to *delivering a consequence* to your teenager. When you do that, something is taken away for a certain time—no use of the car over the weekend, no video games for a week. Remember, with a control battle, teens are continually fighting parental requirements or expectations. Taking something away for a set period of time does nothing to change that. It only builds resentment and lets them believe they are victims of their unreasonable parents. But *earning back privileges* requires a teenager to make a real change, to demonstrate a commitment and a sincere effort to cooperate with and address parental requirements and expectations.

When teens acknowledge the problem, commit to its resolution, and demonstrate sustained good faith effort to address it in an ongoing way, they have reearned privileges. This puts the time frame squarely on the teens, and in the long run, that is exactly what they need to succeed in life—to know that they are in charge of their lives, that they are the masters of their own fates.

I'll show you how this works in real life in the next chapter.

CHAPTER 6

Making the Big Shift

At this point many of my clients say to me, "Okay, this all sounds great in theory, but how do I actually use these concepts in everyday life? How do we change from our usual way of doing things to the new way? After all, Neil, you've explained how powerful the Control Battle Beast can be, how easy it is to keep doing things in the same old ineffective way. I don't know where to begin, or which things to change first!"

In this chapter we will take a closer look at how earned privileges and holding a positive vision of your teen can be put into practice, how to make the big shift away from the control battle–based relationship, and how to keep it from returning.

And once you're out of clutches of the control battle, you can start to enjoy your teenager—and enjoy being a parent again.

The Talk That Kills the Beast

Here is your opportunity to push the "restart" button and initiate the change that will starve the Beast and end the control battle. It's called The Talk.

Before moving forward with The Talk, you need to be fully armed and prepared to make the changes this new way of living requires. This means you must have a strong understanding of the concepts as well as an emotional readiness to take a leadership role and move forward. If you are clear about where you're going, and utilize your skills for ending the control battle, your teen will follow.

Some teens will accept the new arrangement with little resistance, knowing that changes are necessary and that some parental intervention had to be coming. Others will fiercely resist the new order and cling to the status quo.

Some teens may be confused and not know how to proceed. Here is where you will need to uphold that healthy vision of your teenager, know that your teen needs to come around, and trust that that will happen. You will need to bolster your confidence in your own ability to stay positive and emotionally detached from, although empathetic toward, your teen's objections and arguments.

One thing to keep in mind moving forward is that we are talking about changing the relationship patterns in your family. And change, even good change, can be quite scary. Some parents have likened the feeling to bungee cord jumping. In your mind you know you're safe, but at a feeling level, it seems very wrong. So when you change your responses to your teen, it may feel strange and unnatural, and your teen may become upset. You may have a strong urge to remove your teen's discomfort—and *your* discomfort with your *teen's* discomfort. So know this in advance, have faith, and take the leap.

The Talk will begin the shift, moving your relationship out of the control battle. It includes three basic principles:

- using a positive emotional tone,

- having faith in your teen, and

- taking responsibility only for your parenting and leaving the responsibility for your teen's behavior to your teen.

Preparation for The Talk

To prepare for The Talk, make a list of the behaviors—both general and specific—you expect your teenager to change.

A List of Behaviors

Here are some examples of what to present and how you might present it.

- **Make schoolwork a priority.** "This includes completing and doing a good job on all homework assignments, studying for tests, and having regular dedicated homework and studying time with no distractions. I expect you to show me what you're working on and respond respectfully when I ask."

- **Help out around the house.** "This includes participating in nightly kitchen cleanup after dinner before you do anything else. Cleanup includes putting away leftovers; putting dishes in the dishwasher; washing, drying, and putting away pots and pans; wiping the counters and table; and sweeping the floor. If we all work together, this will only take ten or fifteen minutes."

- **Speak to me in a respectful tone of voice, even when you are frustrated, disappointed, or angry.** "Name calling, slamming doors, and breaking things are all unacceptable."

- **Be a good role model to your younger sister.** "Be kind; calling her names and constantly rejecting her is mean and hurtful. When you are busy or simply want alone time, you need to communicate it kindly. You need to find a time and a way to include her, play with her, and help her feel safe and important to you. When she's annoying you and won't stop, ask me for help. Do not hurt her feelings."

A List of Privileges

Now that you've made your list of behaviors that you'd like to see changed, make a list of the privileges that are either at risk or are now suspended, such as

- cell phone,

- use of the car on the weekends, and

- ski trip with friends over spring break.

The Meeting

Okay, now you're ready to have your meeting. This is the time and place where you will have The Talk and make the shift. Arrange a meeting where there are no distractions; TV off and cell phones stashed away, not just set on silent.

1. Begin by describing the problems that you want to discuss. Start with the relationship issues. "There's way too much fighting and negativity in our household." State your concerns. "I'm not seeing the commitment to school that I need to see, and I've been trying to get you to change that, without any success." Or, "I'm not comfortable with the name calling and hurtful way you're treating your brother. I've told you to knock it off, but it keeps happening."

2. As a parent, acknowledge your part in the problem and offer an apology. By admitting you are involved, you model taking responsibility and you avoid the argument about whose fault it is. In fact, we want to stay away from the

concept of fault entirely. Explain that you (the parent) may have given the wrong impression about how things work and may be guilty of arguing, fighting, indulging, and maybe trying too hard to make things work out, which has created conflicts. We must acknowledge that we have not given our teens enough credit for their ability to make their own decisions, change their own behaviors, solve their own problems, and be successful.

3. Next, list many of your teen's strengths, give examples, and express how you admire him or her.

4. Clarify that the things your teen has and the activities he or she enjoys are *privileges* and, like all privileges, must be earned.

5. Make it clear that your teen earned those privileges by virtue of being responsible and having a good attitude in the past (if that's the case), but that because of his or her current lack of responsibility and poor attitude, those privileges are no longer warranted. Add that you know he or she is fully capable of reearning the privileges, but the choice to do what is necessary to earn them at any given time belongs to him or her and not to you.

6. Apologize for not holding your teen to high enough standards and for allowing privileges that are not currently being earned. Explain that by continuing to give these privileges, you are taking away your teen's right to fail. And if teens don't have the right to fail on their own, they can't learn to succeed on their own.

7. State the behaviors you want your teenager to change from the list you made before the meeting. Be sure that you don't try to cover every contingency. The bottom line should always be "as we (the parents) request."

8. Inform your teen of the privileges he or she is now losing or is at risk of losing. In most situations when things have gone far enough to warrant The Talk, privileges should be revoked so that it's clear this isn't just another ineffective discussion with the hope that talking (and not acting) will change things.

The Gap

So you've delivered The Talk. If you've revoked privileges, your teen is going to want to know when they will be given back. That's when you will introduce the concept of the Gap. Your answer is going to be, "You will get your privileges back when you earn them."

The Talk in Action

Let's take a look at an example of how to use The Talk.

Geoff and Will

Geoff (fifteen) and his brother Will (thirteen) enjoy playing video games and competing. Both boys are good students and play sports, but the video games have become an obsession. The only thing the boys seem to think about, talk about, or engage in are their games. They still do their schoolwork, although they rush through it to get to the games. They still go to sports practice, but they rarely talk about the team. On the weekends their friends come over and they have large-scale competitions, including overnight marathons.

Getting Geoff and Will to do any home responsibilities, including cleaning their messes in the kitchen, the game room, and the bedroom, has become a major effort.

The parents get nods, but no follow through. They're hearing this a lot: "We're in the middle of an important game and will do it as soon as we get to the next level." As far as the parents can tell, neither kid has ever made it to the next level!

So the parents have been frustrated for some time now but have been putting up with it for several reasons:

- They're glad their boys are getting along and share a common interest. This is way better than the fighting they used to do!

- They always wanted their house to be the house that all the kids come to. They don't want to ruin that.

- They're glad their sons aren't out using drugs or alcohol.

Geoff and Will are basically good kids, so why start a huge battle? They almost always have friends over, and the parents don't want to make a scene in front of the other kids. Their parents have tried being nice, but that has accomplished nothing. Now it's to the point where there is a battle almost every night and weekend. "Clean this up!" "Put that away!" "Stop the games and do your work!" "Stop the games and go to bed!" Each request elicits the same response: a passive "I will," followed by no action, which is lately followed by "Right now!" After spending an enormous amount of energy, the parents get about half of what they asked for, and then the boys are back to their games.

Breaking point. After what seemed like weeks or months of this, Mom got totally fed up and told her sons: "No more video games for a week."

What happened? Both boys hung out at their friend's house and played their games there. The restrictions made no difference, and three days later their father let them start playing at home again in exchange for some minor cleanups. This didn't go over well with Mom.

When Mom got upset with Dad for "giving in," he said, "Well it wasn't working anyway, so I decided to try something different. At least this achieved *something.*" Three days later, things were back to the same unpleasant normal, except Mom was still angry with Dad, and Dad thought Mom was being unreasonable and should be more supportive of him and the kids.

It was at this point that I received a call from Mom, asking for a consultation. She explained that she and her husband were struggling with their boys, and now with each other, and needed to get on the same page.

During our consultation, we established that the boys' lack of accountability and responsiveness to their parents was indeed a problem and that a control battle with some momentum had developed. The boys were becoming less responsible, and this was affecting their school effort and performance. We acknowledged that both boys were essentially excellent young men with many strengths, but the current problems were overshadowing those strengths and were too unpleasant and destructive to be allowed to go on.

We also established that while both parents agreed there was a problem that needed to be solved regarding the boys, Mom and Dad had also become frustrated with one another because of their different styles of communication. Mom has a tendency to become emotional and sharp when she is upset, whereas Dad tends to avoid intense emotion and conflict. We decided that a "control battle reversal plan" would be ideal because it encouraged a positive tone, which Dad liked, and put the burden of change on the kids, which they both liked, and this helped them feel better about one another, too.

Turning point. That night they sat the boys down and had the following discussion.

Dad: Look, boys. Mom and I aren't happy with the amount of tension and arguing we've all been experiencing together. We're not comfortable with your lack of cooperation and your priority of games over responsibilities.

Will: What's the big deal? We get our work done!

Mom: Please let us continue. You'll get a chance to speak. We know you're great kids: bright, talented, athletic, handsome, and in many ways, thoughtful and responsible. And yes, most of the time you get your schoolwork done, but not up to the best of your ability. And family responsibilities and chores are another story.

Dad: You're teenagers, so I guess a certain amount of ignoring your parents is to be expected. But things have gotten out of hand and there needs to be a serious adjustment here. Mom and I are feeling completely taken for granted, and every request and limit is an enormous battle. We don't want to work that hard.

Mom: I feel like I owe you all an apology. I've been upset with you, so I've been angry and argumentative. That's not how I want to be, and it's not what you need.

Dad: I owe you all an apology as well.

Geoff: You don't yell much, Dad. You've been pretty cool with us.

Dad: That may be true, but it's also true that I haven't been dealing with things. I think I've given you both the impression that I'm okay with your behavior, and I'm not. And you both deserve a father who will be straight with you. Your mom deserves that too.

Mom: So here is what we've concluded. Video gaming is fine with us. Having friends over is fine with us. Here's what's not fine with us: Not doing a thorough job on your homework. Not doing your chores. Saying "okay" when we ask you to do something and then just not doing it.

Will: We can't help it. When you're into a video game, nothing else exists. That's what's so cool about video games.

Mom: That explains a few things, but it's not good enough. We need to be able to talk to you and know you are hearing us.

Dad: So before you go forward with any more gaming, before any friends come over again, and before you go out, there are several things that need to be addressed. First, Mom and I need to know that you understand and agree to uphold the priorities of schoolwork, home responsibilities, and being responsive when Mom or I ask for something. Next, we want a full cleaning of your bedrooms and bathroom. When that is done, Mom and I will review where you are in each of your classes and see where things need to be shored up.

Will: Okay. Geoff, let's get this done fast so we can play this afternoon.

Mom: That's not going to be possible, boys. First we need to know that you get what we're saying. If you both show an excellent attitude and a full effort, Dad and I will consider offering you the privileges you want, but not until we're confident that you have your priorities straight and you demonstrate that to us. Right now is your opportunity to earn them, and earning them is the only way you will get them.

Dad: Like we said, Mom and I know you are both great kids and are fully capable of earning the privileges you want. We will no longer give you privileges that you haven't earned. That's an insult to your ability and we once again apologize for not holding you to the high standards you are capable of.

Did you notice the critical elements in this talk? The parents took responsibility for giving their kids the wrong idea previously and apologized several times. The tone was not at all punitive, and the parents continually emphasized their sons' strengths. They made it clear that they wanted their boys to enjoy their privileges. They clarified their expectations and did not offer a specific time for reinstating privileges. This allowed the Gap to work its magic. By keeping the timing open and the burden of responsibility on their teens, it motivated the boys to change and to address their parents' expectations.

At our follow-up visit a few weeks later, I learned that things had turned around and the boys were back on track. There was still some limit testing going on that required some reinforcing and fine tuning, but the Beast was nowhere to be found.

How Teens Can Fill The Gap

Here are a few more pointers on how teens can "fill the Gap" and reearn their lost privileges. First of all, before you offer a path to earning back privileges, be sure that your teen is open and interested. It's best if the teen asks the question, "What do I need to do?" Otherwise parents run the risk of trying to get their kid to do something, and meeting resistance. That's the structure of a control battle, so let the desire for change come from your teen.

Second, set the bar high enough that it becomes clear to your teen that the privileges only come back and stay in place when he or she is committed to a substantial change. Here are some ideas for effective ways to have kids reearn privileges:

- Have your son or daughter write an essay on the subject of the problem, including what the problem is, why it's a problem, what the correct behavior would be, and what his or her plan is for demonstrating and maintaining the correct behavior. For instance, a boy who has been swearing at his parents might be required to write an essay on verbal abuse. A girl who has been hurtful to a younger sibling could write a report on the effects of bullying and what her plan for change will be. Other essay topics might include drug abuse, responsibility, trust, and communication skills.

- After the essay is written, have your teen discuss it with you in a mature and positive manner. Use this time to have an in-depth discussion on standards and expectations, and take a positive yet authoritative stance. This is an opportunity to recount your teen's strengths and your expectations that his or her best self will be demonstrated.

- When your daughter or son verbalizes acceptance of the standards and expectations with a positive attitude, suggest ways to demonstrate the positive behaviors. These could include focusing on schoolwork, being cooperative and respectful when asked to do something, being kind and giving to a younger sibling, doing some serious housework or gardening, and accepting lost privileges with a good attitude. Once again, do not commit to a time your teen will get his or her privileges back. The teen brain will hear that as a promise. Only commit to a time to discuss progress.

Keeping the Beast at Bay

Now that you've had The Talk and your teenager knows that the privileges must be earned, there's been an enormous change in your family dynamics. You've stopped feeding and paying attention to the Beast, and it's withering away. Now we want to keep it that way.

Ask yourself: "Which of my own behaviors feeds the Beast? Am I being reactive or using a negative tone? Am I easily roped into trying to get my teen to manage her responsibilities? Am I always being a "nice guy" and not holding my kid to high enough standards?" That's where you're going to want to be vigilant about your own behavior. You want to let the Beast go hungry.

In so many control battle–based relationships, parent-teen arguing is at the core. So one thing you want to be careful about is not initiating or getting sucked into an argument. Remember, we all react and argue from time to time. But when we're dealing with the control battle, we want to go that extra mile to avoid feeding the Beast that's been destroying our family. Thankfully, there's a great tool we can use to avoid arguments.

Validation: A Tool to Support the Change

When trying to change a behavior, often it is much harder to *not* do something than it is to *do* something. If parents simply try not to argue, they can only hold out so long before they'll likely give in to the temptation. So here is something that parents can do instead.

Let's stop and consider what fighting really is. Think about a fight you may have had with your partner, for instance, and let's ask the question: what did you and your partner really want? Chances are you both wanted to feel understood, to be validated. You both wanted empathy. These are emotional needs, and getting our emotional needs met is important to all of us. When others take the time to show they care about our feelings, we immediately feel better. In fact, feeling understood and validated can be more important than winning an argument and getting our way.

Validation can be a powerful tool for stopping an argument before it starts. Rather than counter what your teen is saying—in other words, argue—validate your teen's feelings. This is not the same as agreeing with or approving of the way your teen is expressing his or her feelings. It is simply validating the feelings themselves. Therapists and authors Hall and Cook (2010) wrote a wonderful book, *The Power of Validation*, that explains this effective tool to parents. The book is aimed primarily at parents of younger children, yet validation is a powerful tool with preteens, teens, and adults as well.

Let's look at some examples of this concept in action.

Teen: I hate you!

Parent: I hear that and I can see that you're really angry with me.

Teen: You never let me do anything!

Parent: I understand that it's really frustrating when you want to do things and you have to face restrictions.

Teen: Why do I get blamed for everything?

Parent: I hear that you're feeling unfairly blamed for many things. I see where that can be really hurtful.

Teen: Mom, can I go to a sleepover at Amber's house tonight? Gina and Jessica are going too and it's going to be really fun.

Parent: You girls do have a lot of fun together, and I know you really want to go. You've got a soccer game early tomorrow morning and it's not okay to do sleepovers when you have a game the next morning. You might remember the last time we tried it, you were pretty upset with how you played.

So whether your teen is communicating with hostility or respect, in statements or questions, we always have a good option. We can respond in a way that addresses the emotional need behind the words; we can validate.

My wife, Eileen, who works with discipline policy in schools, taught me a great validating tool that she uses. After listening to a teen's explanation for breaking a rule, she'll respond, "That makes perfect sense." Hearing this, the kid will relax and be more open to what follows, which might be, "Unfortunately, that solution didn't seem to work out very well, did it? I wonder if there were any other ways you might have dealt with that." Invariably, a teen will come up with at least one safe, healthy, legal, socially acceptable way of dealing with the situation, thereby avoiding a lecture.

Then, all Eileen needs to do is compliment the teen's solution and brainstorm together how the teen can access that response in a similar situation the next time. The teen will still be facing a school sanction, but will accept it more easily and with a greater likelihood of learning from the experience. This approach works for parents, too.

In several extreme cases I've worked with, the teen would follow the parent (usually a mother) around the house and badger her in an attempt to get what the teen wants: "Why can't I borrow the car? You let Marissa borrow the car. She gets everything. You hate me. You've always loved Marissa more than me. You're just listening to your stupid boyfriend, Roger. Everything was fine until you started listening to him. If you don't let me use the car I'll just move out. What's the point of living with people who hate you?"

The parent would go from room to room trying to get away from the badgering teen. Some mothers have even locked themselves in their bathroom or left the house in an attempt to get away from the badgering.

A technique that's been very successful for parents to address this kind of behavior is getting a pad of paper and a pencil, sitting down facing your teen, and simply writing down what you hear. When your teen asks, "What are you doing?" you reply, "I want to make sure I understand your feelings. I hear what you're asking for, and I'm happy to discuss how you can get what you want, but not when you are badgering me. Badgering is a form of abuse and is not acceptable. When you are ready to apologize and listen and not just talk, I'll be happy to have the conversation."

Let's review the many ways that validation supports our goals. Instead of being reactive, we are being thoughtful and taking charge of our own response to the situation. We are using an empathetic and supportive tone rather than a negative one. Also, we are not being other-person focused. We are not telling our teens what to do or trying to control their behavior. We are starving the Control

Battle Beast and then finally, by being an emotional resource to our kids, we are communicating that we are on their side.

Enjoying Parenting Your Teenager

Congratulations! You've made the big shift and you're committed to developing your skills to stay out of control battles with your teen, regardless of how challenging your teen is making that for you. Now what?

Well, now you get to enjoy parenting your teenager.

We need to remember that adolescence is simply a developmental stage with its own tasks and characteristics. Let's think back to when our teenagers were toddlers and how special and fun that time was. How enthralled they were with everything new; how much they enjoyed us reading to them and playing with them; how much they needed us. And then remember what it was like when they wouldn't go to sleep and demanded more reading, another drink of water, or simply kept getting out of bed.

Every developmental stage has its challenges, but if we expect the challenges, we'll be able to focus on the positives and thoroughly enjoy adolescence as much as the previous stages. And just like when our kids were toddlers, our teenage sons and daughters are going to make plenty of mistakes. We have to be realistic and know that they'll make lots of poor choices that could lead to poor outcomes. And yet they need us to go through these trials and tribulations with them in very much the same way we helped them go to bed when they were toddlers. If we use our skills for ending the control battle, we'll get through the tough times, and we'll be able to create a positive relationship to enjoy together. And the more positive experiences we share with our teenagers, the easier it is to get through the tough times.

Take a minute and reflect on what you might have wanted or needed and perhaps didn't get when *you* were a teenager. Did your parents take the time to understand who you really were, or did they criticize you for not acting the way they expected you to? Did you feel supported in developing your interests and skills? Did they create time to enjoy being with you in fun ways? And when you screwed up, did they help you learn from the experience, or did they simply make you feel bad about yourself? This simple reflection can be a powerful reminder of just how much, and in how many ways, your teenager truly needs you.

As you build your skills for ending the control battle, you actually build a great skill set for enjoying your teen as well. You have a healthy vision of your teenager and faith that he or she will do great in life. You've established high standards and reestablished your parental authority. In addition, you've learned how to validate your teen and avoid arguments. In chapter 2 you learned that teens need excitement and the opportunity to take risks, be creative, and be with other teens, and that the areas and interests teens focus on and invest in will often be there for their lifetimes. Think of some ways you can support, engage, and enjoy your teen in these areas.

One of my sons is a drummer, and my wife and I found ourselves going to punk rock concerts where he was performing. Punk rock would not have been our first choice of a musical genre to listen to, but it allowed us to connect with and enjoy our son and appreciate his talent. I have to confess that I actually ended up enjoying the music.

If your daughter likes to read, read what she reads and discuss it with her. If she plays a sport, do it with her or enjoy watching, photographing, or videoing her. If your son plays video games, play with him or at least be with him while he plays, and have him explain his strategy. Perhaps you're good with auto mechanics and your son is interested in cars. Getting a junker of a car and helping him rebuild it would be a great project for you both. Remember, he'll want to do some of it on his own, which means he'll probably screw some things up. Keep in mind the purpose of the project is learning and connecting, not doing a perfect job.

Because you've reestablished your parental authority, you can now set the standard that your teen must be involved in family activities and other positive social activities beyond simply "hanging out" with friends. In fact, hanging out with friends is a privilege that must be earned as a condition of engaging in more productive uses of time.

So plan family time. Let everyone in the family, including you, have a chance to choose an activity or outing, and involve everyone in the preparation. It may be that you're all going to play video games or go to a skateboard park, but be sure to make the time fun.

Help your kids plan events with friends. If they want friends over to watch movies, help them plan and prepare food and drinks. It may be a good time for you and your teenager to make pizza together and talk.

Helping Your Teenager Learn and Grow

This might be the most important activity of all—just talking and connecting with your teenager. Let's look at how Jake's dad did this.

Jake

Jake wants to go to a huge all-day concert with his friends the Saturday before his finals. Dad knows that Jake needs to study, and the concert would wear him down. It would be easy to say no and just let Jake get upset, argue, and fight. Alternatively, he could discuss the situation with Jake.

Dad: That sounds great, Jake; some of your favorite bands are playing. I'm not sure how that works with finals week, though. I know you've got your big report due and you need a good grade on your math final. What are your thoughts about all that?

Jake: I don't know, I'll get it done. I just want to go; everyone's going.

Dad: Have they got their tickets yet?

Jake: I'm not sure.

Dad: How much are the tickets?

Jake: $120. But it's an all-day concert.

Dad: Do you have $120?

Jake: Yes, but not much more.

Dad: I thought you were saving up for the motorized skateboard. Are you still thinking about that?

Jake: Yeah, but this just came up and I sooooo want to go.

Dad: Sounds like there are some issues to think through. Is this how you really want to spend $120? Would this compromise your report and your math final?

Jake: I'll do fine on my math final and I'll get the report done. Why is everything such a big deal?

Dad: I get that you really want to do this, but before you buy a ticket, I'm going to need to see a timeline for writing your report and preparing for your math final. And if I were you, I'd make sure that your friends actually bought their tickets so you don't end up with an expensive ticket and you're on your own. Make sense?

Jake: (grumpily walking off) I guess so.

In this interaction, Jake went off unhappy with Dad's qualifiers, but it was a lot better than Dad simply saying no and Jake learning nothing. In this case, his father was actually supporting him in figuring things out, and he'll most likely come back with a plan for his report and studying for his math final. Meanwhile, the concert plans will probably fizzle out with his friends, who have their own problems turning this idea into a reality. Dad showed Jake how to think things through and make a plan, and he stayed calm and didn't criticize Jake for his idea.

When Jake was a toddler, his dad needed to teach him to soothe himself and go to sleep. Now that Jake's a teenager, his father needs to help him learn to plan, problem solve, and make good decisions.

Showing interest in your teen's thoughts, feelings, and activities will not only support healthy self-esteem, it will help develop your teen's ability to connect with others, enjoy true adult intimacy throughout life, and also build cognitive skills. Even when your teen is upset and wants to argue, when you slow the interaction down, validate his or her thoughts and feelings, and discuss things at a deeper level, it teaches good thinking and problem-solving skills—skills needed for life.

When we use our skills for ending the control battle and focus on engagement, we strike gold: a rewarding relationship with our teenager.

CHAPTER 7

Self-Esteem and Happiness

Before we go on to part 3 and discuss some specific applications for ending the parent-teen control battle, I'd like to talk about self-esteem and happiness. These are important for our teenagers' healthy development, and when not fully understood, parents who are trying to support their teens can end up in a control battle.

Often parents will call me with concerns about a child, asking if I can provide counseling to help raise their son or daughter's self-esteem. I've sometimes thought that if I could invent some kind of hydraulic self-esteem raiser, I'd be a billionaire! Unfortunately, developing self-esteem is somewhat more complex than simple mechanics.

The Importance of Self-Esteem

Self-esteem is probably the most important element necessary for a child to grow into a happy and emotionally healthy adult. We should want nothing more for our children than for them to thoroughly enjoy being and exploring who they are, enjoy knowing and developing their talents, understand and honor their basic nature, and move safely forward in the world with skill and confidence. This is exactly what self-esteem is: confidence in one's own worth and abilities.

Kids who have low self-esteem, or who feel their self-esteem is being challenged, have a greater tendency to enter into control battles. And the control battle itself can have a negative impact on self-esteem.

As we discussed in chapter 2, during early adolescence a teen's self-esteem is frequently under challenge. Social acceptance is of greater concern than ever before, and kids will work hard to win the approval of their peers. They begin to put their need for approval into the hands of others with similar needs for approval, quite often at the expense of what the parents believe to be their best interests. Children entering adolescence with low self-esteem are at higher risk for self-destructive behavior. For those with high self-esteem, the risk of falling into negative behavior patterns to achieve acceptance and avoid feelings of rejection and failure will be far lower.

How Do We Get It?

We develop self-esteem in two essential ways. First is the way most people think about: growing up in a family and a social environment that recognizes and affirms us—our parents and siblings, extended family, neighborhood, and schools. Because children identify so strongly with their parents, they also believe that the way their parents treat them is a direct reflection of their worth. So if a child feels listened to, and her thoughts and feelings are affirmed, she will see value in her thoughts and feelings. If her thoughts and feelings are not validated by her mom and dad, she will view her own thoughts and feelings as unworthy, and she will see herself as unworthy.

The second way self-esteem is cultivated, one often overlooked by caring parents, is through the development of abilities and achievements. There are many ways for young people to be competent in life, and it's important for them to develop competence according to their own nature and unique potential, whatever that may be.

A tulip bulb can only become a tulip. It will never become an azalea, regardless of how well we water it or fertilize it. It can, however, become a beautiful and healthy tulip if cared for properly. The same is true with people. Young people can be nurtured and supported to develop the potential of their basic nature. When allowed to understand, appreciate, and successfully develop their own potential, they stand tall with self-esteem. When they don't understand or develop their abilities, their self-esteem suffers.

Strong self-esteem encourages self-valuing behavior. Self-valuing behavior creates good feelings and success. Good feelings and success support strong self-esteem. This is a positive self-esteem cycle. Conversely, weak self-esteem can breed low effort and self-destructive behavior. Low effort and self-destructive behavior lead to bad feelings and failure. Bad feelings and failure support weak or low self-esteem, resulting in a negative self-esteem cycle (see figures 1 and 2).

Figure 1. Positive Self-Esteem Cycle

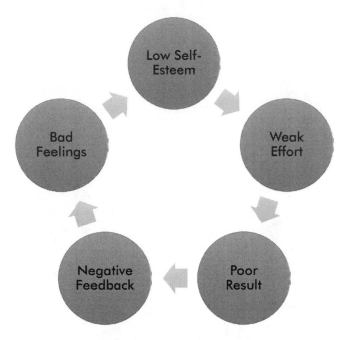

Figure 2. Negative Self-Esteem Cycle

Caring parents often believe that if their children have the first precursor to self-esteem—a positive, loving environment—they will automatically perform up to their potential, and often this turns out to be true. But simply focusing on affirming your child may not be enough to start and maintain the positive self-esteem cycle. Kids also need direction and structure to learn basic life skills for developing their competence. As they develop these critical life skills, they achieve success, work toward their potential, and create strong self-esteem. Eventually, kids can grow and learn to maintain a healthy self-esteem cycle independently.

Ben

Ben is an exceptionally bright adolescent who went through elementary school with ease and success. He was easygoing and got along well with everyone. His teachers liked him and he did passably well in his studies; he caught on very easily and did his work with little effort. However, his teachers reported that Ben's work was sloppy and he didn't always finish it on time. They reassured Ben's parents that he was learning the material, and they weren't terribly concerned.

Ben's parents often felt frustrated that he wouldn't sit down and do his work when they asked him to. He preferred to play games on the computer, and they had a hard time pulling him away from that. When they did, he would read recreationally or play in his room, but he wouldn't get going on his work. When his parents forced him do his homework, Ben resisted, saying it was easy and stupid. They usually succeeded in getting him to do his work, but rarely to a level that represented his true potential. The result was a chronic control battle where Ben's parents were always trying to get him to apply himself, while Ben, rather successfully, resisted their efforts.

Ben's parents figured that Ben was doing okay in school because the teachers liked him and his grades were fine; he liked to read and he showed interest and skill with computers. Even though they would have liked Ben to demonstrate more care in his work, they decided it was probably silly to fight over neatness or timeliness. In fact, because Ben's parents wanted Ben to grow up with high self-esteem, they didn't want to overemphasize the negatives and fight over these issues. They decided to back off so that they wouldn't injure Ben's self-esteem.

By the time Ben reached his freshman year in high school, he was no longer doing so well. He had developed the habit of staying up late and playing computer games, his—and his friends'—only interest and passion. By now, a control battle with his parents was in full swing. Ben's parents constantly struggled with him to manage his schoolwork and to do anything active, such as playing a sport or mountain biking. He was experimenting with marijuana and claimed it enhanced his ability to do his writing assignments. Ben's teachers continued to like him but generally reported that he didn't apply himself. At the end of every grading period, his parents would threaten and fight with him to do his work and catch up. Ben usually had at least one class that he was interested in, and he would get an A in that class, but in his other classes, he would go along with little effort and get C's and sometimes even a D or F.

If we were to ask him, Ben would tell us that he had great self-esteem. He would say it was the adults who had a problem, not him. In truth, Ben had become cynical, no longer valuing himself or those around him. At this point, left to his own devices, Ben was at risk for becoming more seriously involved with drugs and dropping out of school. These are certainly not self-valuing behaviors and do not signal healthy self-esteem.

So what went wrong? Ben's parents loved and cared for him. They acknowledged and supported his areas of strength. They bought him a computer, and they allowed him to be himself. Yet Ben got caught in a negative self-esteem cycle. He was not developing his potential, and his behavior became self-destructive and oppositional.

It was obvious to everyone that Ben had terrific potential, but he was not held accountable or properly supported to develop that potential. Because he was so bright, the problems were easily overlooked, at least initially. Like all kids, he needed to learn to do his best, regardless of what that "best" was. Ben was failing to develop his potential because his parents and teachers did not maintain high enough standards for him. He received the love and support he needed, but not the structure and challenge he needed to develop his abilities. Consequently, Ben never developed real self-esteem. Eventually, the control battle further eroded Ben's self-esteem and left his parents feeling helpless to parent him effectively.

High Standards

There are many reasons to insist upon high standards for our kids. Holding high standards helps them see how well they can do. They learn to persevere through the difficult part of learning and come out victorious on the other side. It teaches them that they can dig deeply into themselves and accomplish something that they might not have believed they could, so they learn to believe in themselves. Often when I see a teen with low self-esteem and no areas of achievement to feel good about, his parents will say, "I don't know what happened; he just never stuck with anything." Struggling to learn the piano can be very difficult, but after working on it each day for only thirty minutes or so, what used to be difficult will eventually become easy, and we will be ready to face a new, more difficult phase of learning, while enjoying our gradually acquired musical skills.

The same can be said for learning a sport, or any physical activity, as well as gaining proficiency in art, foreign languages, mathematics, social and emotional skills, and any other area of knowledge or skill we can imagine. Whether or not we are naturally gifted at something, by setting goals and working at it, with appropriate direction and support, over time we will achieve success.

Once our kids learn that they can begin something with relatively low skill and knowledge, and by persevering, eventually achieve success, they will have a critical skill for life that will bring them confidence and stronger self-esteem. Young people who are confident in their ability to achieve are far less likely to enter into control battles with their parents, because when they are asked to do their work, regardless of what it is, they have learned that work pays off and they resist it less.

When Are Standards High Enough?

An appropriately high standard is the expectation that your teenager will put in a solid effort with a positive attitude. Putting in the time is important, yet if she's doing so with a careless "this sucks" attitude, with little regard for the quality, that's not meeting a high standard.

A general rule of thumb for setting an appropriately high standard for schoolwork could be one grade above what your teen could easily get. If she can get C's with little effort, an appropriately high standard could be B's. If she can get B's easily, she should go for A's, and if she can easily get A's, she should push further in some other way—perhaps a self-directed project in one of her classes, a job, or extra classes at the local college.

It's best if kids involve themselves in an organized activity beyond schoolwork, and, once again, put in the time with a good attitude. The extracurricular activity can be a club, organization, or team (in or out of school), a job, or a family responsibility such as helping the family business or providing child care to siblings.

Once kids join something, under most conditions they should be required to stay with it and give it their best. The old saying "A job worth doing is a job worth doing well" is a great value to teach. That way, regardless of what they're doing, they'll end up feeling good about it, and about themselves.

When Are Standards Too Rigid or Too High?

The control battle can occur not only when standards are set too low, but also when they're too specific, rigid, or high. Remember, we establish high standards to help our kids discover their potential and to feel good enough about themselves to persevere through difficulties. If we stress our kids out by requiring all A's so they can get into a specific top college, we will only undermine their self-esteem. Instead of learning to enjoy challenges, they will get the message that it isn't about the challenge, it's about winning, getting the top grade, getting into the best school, getting ahead of the other guy. In other words, it isn't about who they are, it's about an external definition of success.

When are standards too rigid or too high? When they are no longer about making the effort, learning, and growing, but instead are all about a specific outcome, for instance a 4.5 GPA, or winning some specific award or honor. Standards are too high when extreme amounts of time are required day in and day out to succeed. Standards are too high when the struggle to meet them takes away from a balanced lifestyle, when a teenager is no longer involved in the choice to participate in an activity, or when a teenager is constantly stressed and worried about how well he will do.

Support to Succeed

Some kids have an easier time developing their potential than others. They have the gifts of focus, motivation, initiative, and drive. Others may be just as bright but lack these natural personality traits. They may be distractible, noncompetitive, easygoing, and not particularly self-directed. Often these kids are called "lazy" or are otherwise seen in a negative light. Actually, these easygoing traits are very healthy in many social and vocational environments. But they don't work well in most school environments, and teachers and parents can become frustrated and angry with these kids. They need support and structure to succeed and to develop their potential, academic or otherwise.

So along with appropriately high standards, your teen may need certain support structures in place to be successful. If she lacks organizational skills and you expect her to do a great job on her project, she might need your help to put a plan in place that will help her get organized. If we establish high standards and then leave our teens to their own devices, they can feel hopeless and abandoned.

If you help your teen develop a plan and monitor progress, it will ensure success, teach important skills, and show that you truly care. With the good feelings of success, improved organizational skills, and feeling supported by you, your teen will be empowered and motivated to be successful in her next endeavor.

Happiness

Let's talk about happiness. Believe it or not, a teen's lack of happiness can become the starting point of a control battle. You can buy your kid something he wants to own, cook him something he likes to eat, take him someplace he wants to go, give him permission to do something he wants to do, or offer him emotional support when he's down. Some might appreciate it and be truly grateful, while others might take it for granted and have an attitude of entitlement. Under most circumstances, doing nice things for your child is a positive and good thing. It is important to remember, however, that *you* can't make your child happy.

We can create the opportunity for our kids to make themselves happy. We can give them love, support, guidance, limits, and access to resources. But it is up to our kids to discover the path to their own happiness. When parents want their kids to be happy more than the kids want to make *themselves* happy, the stage is set to grow a control battle.

So where, exactly, does happiness come from? How do we find happiness, and how does your child find happiness?

A certain amount of happiness seems to be innate. Some people are born with happy dispositions. They wake up singing, and they cruise along with excitement about their lives, their friends, their activities, and their futures. Negatives seem to roll off their backs. Sure, sometimes they're sad, disappointed, hurt, frustrated, or angry, just like the rest of us. But it seems that under most circumstances, they will be happy.

Many people, though, have a harder time arriving at a state of happiness. For some, just getting up in the morning seems like a burden. Seemingly minor frustrations can cause strong negative emotional responses. Major frustrations can be overwhelming and send an individual into a crisis. Unless they learn the specific skill set necessary to manage their emotions, this group will have a harder time in life.

So what *is* the skill set for happiness?

Before we discuss the skills, let's reaffirm the notion that *you can't make your child happy*. When you try, you are being "other-person focused," and we know where that leads. However, you *can* love your children, enjoy them, demonstrate faith in them, coach them, and set limits with them. You can empower your kids to make themselves happy, even though at any given moment, they may not choose to do so. And do not forget the one person you *can* make happy: *you*. By doing the things necessary for you to be happy, you'll have lots of energy left over for parenting, and you'll be setting a great example for your teenager.

Anita

Let's look at the story of Anita, an eleven-year-old fifth grader, and her parents. (We'll meet Anita again as a teen-ager in the next chapter on depression.) Anita was a bright and talented girl who did reasonably well in school. She could write and draw very well for her age. She was also shy, sensitive, and introverted. Her mom and dad, on the other hand, were very outgoing and social. They had a hard time understanding why Anita wasn't thrilled to be part of the large group activities they loved to experience with family and friends.

"What's the matter with you? Why do you always want to be unhappy?" they would ask their daughter. They didn't understand that large group activities were stressful for Anita. She needed a lot more quiet time alone than they could relate to, so it became a source of stress between Anita and her parents that Anita wasn't upbeat and outgoing.

Her parents tried everything they could think of to make her happy. They bought her things she liked, and she would seem happy for a while, but then she would return to her usual state. Her parents constantly encouraged her to socialize with friends and sign up for group lessons and activities, saying, "Come on, Anita, you'll love it and enjoy yourself. All the girls in your class will be there."

"I don't like the girls in my class," she'd reply. "They're all gossipy and they don't include me."

"Maybe if you tried harder, and made an effort to be nice, they'd include you more!"

And so a control battle was born. Anita became the voice of "no," as her parents were the voice of "yes." Anita's parents supported, encouraged, and sometimes bribed Anita to do the things they thought would be positive for her, and Anita constantly resisted their efforts. The more they encouraged, the more she refused. In fact, Anita actually became less social, more withdrawn, and more isolated—more truly unhappy. One could say that Anita's parents had put themselves in charge of making Anita happy, and Anita put herself in charge of resisting their efforts, staying unhappy.

Happiness Skills

The subject of happiness skills can become very philosophical and even spiritual, but let's be practical and think in terms of what we need to teach our children to be able to create happiness for themselves. Here are some key practices to cultivate.

Self-Knowledge and Self-Acceptance

Our kids all have unique personalities, skills, and interests. Whether an individual is athletic, musical, introverted, or outgoing, we all have different strengths. Nobody is good at everything, but everybody is good at many things. Kids need to know this about themselves and become comfortable with who they are. Whatever their personal combination of traits, they need to be secure enough to invest in and develop their strengths, and to accept themselves but be willing to improve in their areas of relative weakness.

For example, if Anita is artistically inclined, she needs to create art, take art classes, and connect with other kids who are into art. Anita needs to accept that she doesn't have to be the most popular girl in class, she just needs a couple of friends to be close to and to do things with. Anita also needs to learn to get along with the other girls, even though she might not want to spend extra time with them.

Passion and Goals

Another important piece of the happiness puzzle involves passion and working toward goals. It matters less *what* a person is passionate about—because that can change over time. It simply matters that a person *is* passionate. When people are passionate, it gives energy, meaning, and focus to their lives. The energy that passion generates in one aspect of a person's life can spread to other aspects of life. It can be passion that drives us to set and achieve goals, or it can be our goals that help us create passion.

For instance, your son complains of being bored, so you encourage him to join the track team. He reluctantly agrees, and suddenly he's part of a team, a group of kids who are all trying to get to the state meet together, taking bus rides and overnight trips to compete. Quickly, the boredom passes, your son is exchanging texts with new friends, and he now has goals—and passion!—back in his life. With passion, each day has energy, excitement, and focus. Without passion, life can be flat and routines can be boring.

Goals can be personal goals, or group goals—and with teens, both are important. A personal goal might be to win a significant role in the school play, make the varsity baseball team, get into a first choice college, or simply do an advanced trick on a skate-board. A group goal for your teen could be to help build a fabulous float for the homecoming game, win a soccer championship, or pull off a great performance with her band at the talent show.

Personal goals are important because they inspire us to map our way forward. Even if a personal goal for a teen is just to reach level 12 on a video game, it sets the stage in adulthood for making and achieving job or career goals.

Group goals are important for teens because they create bonds that can last a lifetime. Group goals bring an energy that spreads to all the participants and allows them to feel success in the outcome, regardless of their role. After the final performance of the school play, those who worked on the set or sewed the cos-tumes are glowing with success right along with the stars of the show. Group goals teach leadership and many other social skills that are critical to happiness and success in life. Additionally, school-related group goals help bond teens to their school com-munities and encourage academic success.

Emotional Management Skills

For some kids, feeling the range of emotions or feelings is a normal part of their experience. They expect to have feelings and emotions and know that there are positive ones as well as less enjoyable ones, and sometimes they can have both kinds at the same time. They can talk about them, write about them, think about them, and generally figure out what they want to do about them. For others, feelings are barely on their radar. They may not know how to talk or write about their feelings, or they may not even know what they are. Unpleasant feelings may be experienced and expressed as anger or depression. When they don't understand their feelings, they won't know what to do for themselves or how to communicate their feelings or emotional needs to others. Feelings can throw them into a tizzy, and they—and those around them—can become victims of those feelings!

So critical to happiness is the ability to identify feelings, get support from others, and self-soothe; in other words, to know how to calm ourselves down when we become emotional. Self-soothing can be a very individual thing. Common healthy ways that adults self-soothe their upset feelings include working in the garden; any kind of exercise, such as going for a long walk or jog, bike riding, or yoga; meditating; drawing; working on a project; or even cleaning the house. For your teen, self-soothing can be listening to music, shooting baskets, playing a musical instrument, skateboarding, getting lost in a book—the list is endless. The point is that kids and adults alike need to know that when they experience strong, unpleasant feelings, they can recognize them for what they are and do something positive for themselves. And teens need to learn that circumstances will change, time will pass, and the painful feelings will pass as well.

Managing Responsibilities

I don't need to tell you that we all have to do things we would rather not do. Whether these are routine chores such as cleaning the house or completing monthly reports at work, they will always be there. For teens, it might be homework, cleaning their room, or giving a report in front of the class. If they can take these things in stride, and even find something good about them, they will get through them fairly easily, and life will go on to more pleasant things. But if responsibilities aren't addressed in a timely way, problems develop and eventually compound themselves, creating a hole that they will need to find a way out of. Dealing with the consequences of not managing responsibilities requires more energy than dealing with the responsibilities in the first place—and generally offers less reward. Getting in the habit of taking ten minutes to straighten up a bedroom at the end of the day allows a person to stay organized and avoid having to take half a day to clean up a major mess or look for lost car keys. Doing school assignments every day for an hour or two results in better grades and less stress than having to make up work at the end of the semester and spending several intense weekends trying not to fail.

Relationship Skills

Another huge component of happiness and self-esteem is the ability to get along with other people. The subject of relationship skills is enormous and complicated. After all, we are in relationships of many kinds and our ability to manage all those relationships productively is vital to our happiness. Learning how to get along with people, choosing and cultivating friendships, establishing and communicating our boundaries, as well as respecting the boundaries of others, are all important.

And there's more. We all have to learn how to respect authority, knowing how and when to lead and when to follow.

None of us, even as adults, are finished products. We are always in the process of developing skills to effectively manage conflict, to manage intimacy, and ultimately, to create emotionally satisfying relationships.

Our teens feel an enormous pull to be with their peers. That's natural and healthy. It's the only way they will gain proficiency in all these different skills that are vital to their happiness. Understanding this, we can expect that at least part of the time, when relationships disappoint, your teen will be unhappy. That's also natural and healthy and challenges them to use their emotional management skills.

Faith That Things Will Come Out Okay

Happiness requires faith that things will come out okay. Having a generally optimistic attitude is a critical leverage point for happiness. Our kids face many unknowns each and every day. If they get upset and overfocus on what has gone wrong or what might go wrong in the future, every situation will look like a disaster. If, on the other hand, we teach our kids to accept that even though things won't always go the way they want them to go, and they don't know exactly how things will turn out, life will be a great adventure—they'll be able to handle whatever comes up, find the good in the outcome, and be ready for the next phase of that adventure called "life."

Our teens are on a learning curve with all of these happiness skills, and they're not ready to fly solo yet. But that's okay—they still have us to rely on. We can't force these skills on them any more than we can make them happy. That would be just another opportunity to "feed the Beast." What we can do is be there to support them, guide them, and set limits for them. By using our parenting skills and demonstrating faith in our teens' ability to learn and grow, they will eventually go on to lead happy, independent lives.

PART THREE

APPLICATIONS

CHAPTER 8

What if My Teenager Is Depressed?

You may be wondering why we need to talk about depression in a book about parent-teen control battles. Before we dive into that, let's take a look at what depression is and is not.

Depression can most succinctly be described as a pervasive unhappiness with a lack of motivation or enthusiasm for life. The Substance Abuse and Mental Health Services Administration estimates that 11.4% of adolescents age 12 to 17 experienced a major depressive episode in 2014 (Center for Behavioral Health Statistics and Quality 2015). We can therefore assume that depression is going to be a problem for many teens and their families at some point during their adolescence. When people are depressed, they feel removed from those around them, like they're alone in a fog and unable to see anything beyond it. They most often lack energy, and doing even small things can take a lot of effort. To depression sufferers, it seems as if they will always feel this way. They often lack motivation to change anything, having little faith that they'll ever feel better, no matter what they do.

Depression can take many forms. The most obvious symptoms are a tendency to isolate oneself, a loss of interest in previously enjoyed activities and friendships, and extreme sadness—often with long periods of crying. Other symptoms include a loss of appetite or overeating, difficulty or increased sleeping, chronic fatigue, physical ailments, and, at its most extreme, suicidal thinking and behavior. Often, particularly among adolescents, other conditions and behaviors co-occur with depression such as anorexia or bulimia, substance abuse, promiscuity, and self-cutting.

Is It Sadness or Depression?

All of us can be sad or moody from time to time. Sadness is a normal emotional reaction when something bad happens, such as when your teenager's best friend suddenly becomes someone else's best friend and your teen is shunned, or when a kid doesn't get selected to make the team, doesn't get a major role in the school play, or doesn't get invited to the parties that the other kids are being invited to. All these things are hurtful and can cause sadness. But when the sadness is ongoing, lasting weeks instead of days, and begins to interfere with the teen's daily life, then it could be depression.

Any kind of loss can cause extreme sadness. Whether the loss is of a family member, a friend, or a pet, a child or teen will quite naturally experience grief. However, if the grief reaction becomes chronic, it can signal depression.

Where Does Depression Come From?

Several factors contribute to the onset of depression, and though these apply to children, teens, and adults, let's talk about them primarily from the perspective of adolescence.

Low self-esteem. Low self-esteem makes teens more emotionally susceptible to rejection, hurt, and dwelling on personal failures. It interferes with taking healthy risks and making self-valuing personal choices. Low self-esteem encourages self-destructive choices including poor social choices, low effort, and substance abuse, all leading to or increasing depression.

A lack of social-emotional support. Kids need to feel understood, validated, and supported for who they are and what they feel. They need recognition for their accomplishments. Without that, they'll feel disconnected, isolated, and alone.

A lack of physical activity. As we talked about in the section on happiness in chapter 7, physical activity is vital to a healthy mood and brain. Without it, depression is more likely to occur, and less likely to abate.

A lack of perceived empowerment. Teens need opportunities to set and achieve personal goals. It's vital for them to know that regardless of what they choose to do, they can pursue their goals. They need to know that there is a real opportunity for them to achieve and be successful in any environment in which they are placed: school, sports team, home, job, or camp. When students are placed in environments where their best efforts are likely to repeatedly fail, or the expectations are unreasonably high, they can experience chronic stress, and that will commonly lead to depression.

Trauma. Any highly stressful event that leaves a person feeling unsafe, helpless, and not having control over the situation can be traumatic. And a primary symptom of trauma is depression. When kids are exposed to physical or verbal violence, a severe traffic accident, the sudden death of a loved one, sexual abuse, or violence in their neighborhood or home, they will commonly experience depression.

Genetics. Individuals who have a family history of depression can be more susceptible to depression.

Just reading all this might be enough to depress a parent. Yet there is reason to be optimistic. Although depression is very serious, it is also very treatable. With high-quality professional help, and with our help developing our teens' "happiness skills" described in the previous chapter, teens can come through their depression and thrive.

Control Battles and Depression

The control battle itself can cause or contribute to depression. As we discussed in chapter 1, when the Control Battle Beast is thriving in a family, it has a negative impact that can play out in a variety of ways, including depression, in any member of the family. In the case of parents, depression can be the result of worry and burnout; in the case of siblings, it might come out of stress and feeling unimportant in the family; and for the teenager directly involved in the control battle, depression can arise from feeling criticized, alienated, and unable to be successful. These are very serious situations. Fortunately, when skills for ending the control battle are applied and we starve the Beast, depression will leave with the Beast and life can go forward in a healthy way.

Sometimes, however, teenage depression will be the centerpiece of a control battle. When a teenager becomes depressed, it's vital that action be taken to address the situation, and informed and caring parents will do just that. Unfortunately, many professional approaches for treating teen depression relegate the parents to a marginalized role in the treatment, disempowering them from being the resource their teenager needs. Many therapists will work with a teenager individually and perhaps give the parents only updates or pieces of advice, outside of the presence of the teenager. The parents will view the therapist as the person who holds the key to curing their teenager's depression, and will miss how important it is that they remain actively involved.

Another disempowering "solution" is when parents take their teen to a physician who simply prescribes an antidepressant medication as the first response without requiring or even recommending counseling.

Many therapists and physicians work beautifully and effectively with teenagers and their families. Unfortunately, there are also many who will utilize medication or individual therapy without taking the time to understand the context: the family dynamics that relate to the problem and its solution. The unintentional undermining of the parental role leaves the teenager without the primary resource needed to return to a healthy crossing of his or her developmental footbridge.

Anita (Revisited)

Let's see how this happened with Anita, the shy, quiet girl from chapter 7 whose parents kept trying to make her happier. The more they tried, the more Anita resisted until they had established a robust control battle. Anita's parents had become in charge of making Anita happy, and Anita was in charge of them failing to make her happy.

Anita found middle school and the cliques and social stressors very hard to deal with. By the time Anita was a fifteen-year-old high school freshman, she had developed a very negative identity; she socialized with boys and girls who wore only black, symbolic of their identification with all things dark and depressing. She had a seventeen-year-old boyfriend who went to an alternative school for at-risk youth. Anita's parents discovered that she had been superficially cutting herself, which alerted them that professional help was needed. They got Anita into therapy with a well-respected therapist who recommended a psychiatric evaluation. Although they were skeptical about medication, they went along with the recommendation for Anita to begin taking an antidepressant. After a while, they did notice an improvement; Anita was less negative at home and did come to some meals, but she still retreated quickly to her room. There were good days and bad days during the first half of her freshman year, and concern for Anita was still foremost in her parents' minds. They had disciplined her for smoking marijuana and some alcohol use.

There was one frightening occasion when they allowed her to go to a concert and sleep at a friend's house, only to receive a call from one of Anita's friends that she was extremely drunk and had passed out, no adult was there, and they were worried. Her parents picked Anita up and took her to the hospital emergency room, where she was observed for several hours and then sent home.

Anita's parents were extremely upset. They grounded her for a month, but they did let her boyfriend come over and spend time at the house because they were afraid that isolation would only increase their daughter's depression.

Anita's parents were constantly trying to find a balance between allowing privileges so that Anita wouldn't be depressed, and withholding privileges because Anita abused them or wasn't managing her responsibilities. Very little, in fact, had changed since the fifth grade. Anita's parents still acted from the belief that they were in charge of making her happy—and Anita seemed to be in charge of resisting them and making herself unhappy! This was the essential structure of their control battle.

After hearing me speak at their daughter's high school, Anita's parents called for a consultation and I invited them all to come in together. I listened carefully to each of their stories. From Anita I learned how strict and controlling her parents were, and from her parents I heard how hard they tried to make things nice for Anita, who never appreciated anything. Anita's parents wanted to know if Anita was ever going to get over her depression and move forward in life. Were they ever going to be able to stop worrying about her?

I explained to Anita and her parents that the way things were going, the answer was no. As long as Anita's parents were responsible for Anita's happiness and Anita was not, Anita would be depressed and continue to make self-destructive decisions. Anita responded, "I can't help it that I'm depressed!" and her parents went silent, waiting for my response. This was the proverbial "elephant in the room"; the depression was in charge, not Anita. I empathized with and validated Anita's struggle with depression. Depression can be extremely debilitating, and I conveyed a deep understanding of that to Anita and her parents.

Neil: Anita, I get it that depression is no fun at all, but what is your plan for curing it?

Anita: I'm going to therapy and taking antidepressants. What else am I supposed to do?

Neil: It's excellent that you are taking action to treat your depression, Anita. What have you and your therapist worked out for your plan? I know your therapist, and although we haven't discussed your case, I'm sure she's given you lots of ideas to help yourself.

Anita: Yeah, well I do them sometimes, but sometimes I'm too depressed and I just don't feel like it.

Mom: I don't think I've heard about this. What are you supposed to be doing to help yourself?

Anita: She says I'm supposed to get exercise and take an afterschool art class. I go for walks once in a while, but it doesn't help much. I called the art school once but they weren't starting a new class for a month or so.

Mom: And so? Did you sign up for the next class?

Anita: No. I forgot about it. It was too far off. Besides, I just like to do art with my friends. We hang out and draw and I do plenty of art, I don't need to go to a class and do more. I don't even know those people in the class.

Dad: Anita, I don't know what the point of going to therapy is if you're not going to listen to the therapist's advice.

Anita: I like my counselor, but I don't get how going to an art class is going to cure my depression.

Neil: The way you're thinking about things, Anita, you're likely to stay pretty stuck. It sounds like you and your parents are being held hostage to the depression.

Mom: That's exactly how we feel. Is there anything we can do?

Neil: Yes, there is. Depression is very treatable.

I drew this diagram on the whiteboard (see figure 3) and explained:

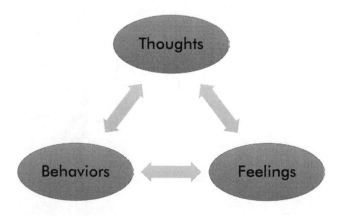

Figure 3. The Thoughts, Feelings, and Behaviors Triangle

Thoughts, feelings, and behaviors all affect, and are affected by, each other. In other words, how we *feel* affects how we think and how we behave. How we *behave* affects how we think and feel, and how we *think* affects how we feel and behave! You may notice that we can control our behaviors, and we can even turn negative thoughts into positive ones if we try. The one area we don't have direct control over is our feelings.

Neil: (continuing) Anita, I'm sure that if you could just decide to feel good and feel happy, you would do just that—wouldn't you?

Anita: Duh. What do you think?

Neil: But think about it: if your feelings are negative, but you surround your negative feelings with positive thinking and positive behavior, eventually your feelings will come around. If you want to *feel* better, you have to choose both positive thinking and positive behavior. Right now, the depression is running the show.

Mom: Wow, that makes sense, and it's in line with what *we've* been saying too—but if Anita doesn't do any of this, what can we do?

Neil: First of all, I think we all have to realize that Anita is a bright, talented, terrific young woman who has not matured yet in this area, that is, in the area of emotional maturity. And it is with emotional maturity that Anita will find happiness. It will come with the development of her ability to manage her thinking, her attitude, and her behavior so that she can make herself happy and successful. It's a learning process.

Anita is perfectly capable of doing this. She may need support, structure, and guidance until she gets the hang of it, but she has all the equipment she needs.

I went on to explain to Anita and her parents that they can't give Anita privileges to make her happy; rather, they should make Anita's happiness strictly Anita's job, and they need to hold her accountable to a positive attitude (thinking) and positive behavior. In alignment with her therapist's advice, Anita needed to be involved in regular, structured activities and get regular exercise. I advised her parents that the only way it would make sense for Anita to be allowed to go to a concert, or to be given significant independent time, was if she had demonstrated the ability to choose healthy behavior and maintain a good attitude. After all, how does it make sense to send a fifteen-year-old girl (who reports that she's too depressed to be responsible for her actions!) to a concert with plenty of opportunity for self-destructive behavior? On the other hand, as Anita began to show a positive attitude and the ability to choose self-valuing behaviors, and as she began to take responsibility for her choices, there could be lots of opportunities for those kinds of activities.

Anita and her parents agreed that several changes must take place in order for Anita to have basic privileges such as the use of her cell phone, the computer (for anything other than schoolwork), and spending time with her friends on weekends.

Anita enrolled in an afterschool art class and attended a yoga class three times a week. Sometimes her mom went with her, and sometimes a friend came, but she had to maintain the three-times-a-week schedule, no matter what.

Additionally, Anita was required to put away her cell phone and join the family for dinner with a positive attitude every night and participate in either the preparing of the meal or the cleaning up.

Several months later, Anita seemed like a different person. She was producing some amazing pieces in her art class, and the teacher selected several of them for a prominent art exhibit. Anita became quite proficient at yoga and was helping her mother learn the poses. She reported that she had come to rely on yoga to settle herself emotionally after all the socializing that was stressful for her during the day. Anita's school performance became a lot more consistent. After some time had passed, and with a clear understanding of the "no drugs or alcohol" policy, Anita was allowed to go to a concert with her friends, and this time, there was no crisis.

So what happened?

What happened was that the family starved their Beast and ended their control battle. Anita's parents stopped being responsible for Anita's happiness and started being responsible for their parenting. While holding a healthy vision of Anita, they created appropriate standards to which she was held accountable. Anita stopped fighting her parents with her depression, and focused on healthy goals and activities. Anita's parents could finally say they weren't fighting with Anita, and they were no longer intimidated by her depression. They all felt like they were on the same side and working for the same goals, but with different roles and jobs.

Depressed teens will tend to look and act quite unhappy. As a result, caring, sympathetic parents who want to help can easily find themselves frustrated and locked in a control battle with their teen and their teen's depression, like Anita and her parents. Because Anita was in individual counseling and taking medication, her parents felt that she was doing everything she could for herself, and they backed off. This left them feeling helpless to be the parents that their daughter needed them to be.

Counseling that supports and guides the family as well as the teen can be a vital resource when it comes to ending the family's control battle, helping the teenager out of depression and back on the healthy journey of self-discovery. (For more information about counseling, please visit http://www.newharbinger.com/34244 and read the online chapter "Should I Consider Counseling?") In Anita's case, family therapy helped the parents end their quest to make their daughter happy and refocused their efforts on holding her accountable to the standards of behavior that Anita needed in order to feel better.

Depression is a very treatable condition when parents are a critical part of the solution. If your teen is depressed, it's important to know that although you can't make your teenager happy, you can provide the loving structure and support vital to your son or daughter's recovery.

CHAPTER 9

Learning Disabilities and ADHD

Learning disabilities (LD) and attention-deficit/hyperactivity disorder (ADHD) are often hidden issues that contribute to the parent-teen control battle. It is very difficult to determine the exact percentage of the population affected by these conditions, given the different criteria for diagnosis of LD from state to state and the subjective nature of ADHD diagnosis. In 2011, approximately 4.7% of public school children in the United States were receiving services for LD (U.S. Department of Education, National Center for Education Statistics 2015) and 11% had at some time been diagnosed with ADHD (Visser et al. 2014). When not identified and addressed, or even when they are, these conditions can make it tough to keep the Beast at bay.

Let's take a brief look at some of the many information-management functions a brain needs to perform to enable kids to be successful in school. The brain needs a way to receive information, store it, access it when it's needed, and then express it. In children and teens with LD, these operations are often less than seamless, resulting in difficulty understanding what is presented, quickly and accurately recalling what they know from memory, correctly remembering the order of things, and breaking tasks down into smaller, more manageable steps so they can be completed. Students who have persistent difficulties acquiring and demonstrating academic skills can be diagnosed with a specific learning disorder in the area of reading, written expression, or mathematics.

ADHD is a condition characterized by three basic issues: difficulties with focus or paying attention, a strong tendency to act impulsively, and hyperactivity. Some kids who are diagnosed with ADHD are more affected by issues of attention and focus, while others are more challenged with hyperactivity and impulsivity.

Difficulties with focus and attention can include distractibility and difficulty paying attention and staying on task. For kids with this characteristic, virtually anything can be a source of distraction—their own thoughts, a body sensation, movement in the classroom, and more. Another aspect of attention issues is hyperfocusing, which refers to concentrating on something so intently that it results in difficulty noticing one's surroundings or pulling away from an activity when it's time to stop. Video games, for instance, have a hyperfocusing effect on many people. Hyperfocusing can make switching from task to task quite difficult. Because kids with this issue can under- or overfocus, we can think of this characteristic as a difficulty managing or being in charge of one's focus.

Impulsivity, as the term implies, is the strong tendency to act on impulse without considering whether or not it's a good idea. As noted in chapter 2, impulsive actions can be a significant issue for many teens. So when this characteristic is part of the syndrome of ADHD, problems can be even more extreme.

With hyperactivity, an individual simply cannot sit still for very long and will have a very strong tendency to fidget and move.

Attention-deficit/hyperactivity disorder is a medical term for a disorder. However, while there are specific brain function differences in individuals with ADHD, we don't have to view this as a disorder. We can see it as simply a difference in traits: traits that have been genetically selected for tens of thousands of years. Often individuals with LD and ADHD observe things that others miss, and they can be extremely creative. Lara Honos-Webb (2010) has written an excellent book entitled "The Gift of ADHD," in which she celebrates the syndrome, reveals many of its positive attributes, and suggests healthy ways to improve functioning and school success.

The Challenges of LD and ADHD

LD and ADHD share many of the same symptoms. Teens with these issues tend to perform below their potential or true ability. LD and ADHD create certain challenges in both school and home environments. Difficulty getting started on schoolwork, finishing work, staying on task, following directions, organizing work and the workspace, and remembering to turn work in on time can all be common problems for kids with ADHD and LD. Because of this, they can seem uncooperative, unmotivated, sloppy, insensitive, self-centered, or otherwise difficult.

Injured Self-Image

If these issues are not assessed and addressed, a teen's underperformance can look like an unwillingness to cooperate. In fact, the effects of living with LD and ADHD can be very demotivating for kids. Imagine going to school every day and constantly struggling to understand what's going on, or struggling to express your knowledge when you *do* understand. Facing schoolwork can become onerous and unrewarding. It's easy for a kid to conclude that she isn't smart or is incapable.

Being perceived as the chronic source of parental dissatisfaction can injure a child or teen's self-esteem as well. After struggling with this for some time, and having their best efforts come up short, kids with LD and ADHD can simply feel like failures and eventually quit trying. And this complicates things because teachers and parents then have a hard time differentiating between ability and effort.

The Control Battle Begins

Really bright kids can often do quite well in spite of their LD or ADHD. When this is the case, their LD or ADHD can be missed entirely. Then, when their condition does begin to limit their performance, parents and teachers focus on what they mistakenly consider to be a lack of cooperation and motivation. This is where the control battle begins to develop!

Let's say a child has done well in elementary school and is considered bright and capable. When he enters adolescence and moves from elementary to middle school, the work becomes more challenging and the need to be organized is beyond his ability. This kid's performance will go down, his sense of futility will go up, and his willingness to apply himself may diminish. At this point his teachers and parents become upset with him, labeling him lazy and oppositional.

"He has the ability. He just doesn't apply himself."

"She disrupts others in the class."

"He spends his time looking out the window instead of doing his work."

"She's constantly interrupting."

"He needs to be the center of attention."

"Her work is messy and incomplete. She just doesn't care!"

This negative labeling is further demotivating and creates greater resistance. The cycle of fighting and punishment becomes the defining characteristic of the parent-teen relationship, and a Control Battle is born.

If you suspect that your child or teen has learning disabilities or ADHD, or you can't figure out why he isn't doing as well as you think he should be, speak with his teacher or school counselor. Schools assess for these conditions and offer resources and recommendations. An alternative to school assessment and services is working with an independent educational consultant specifically trained to provide assessment, educational therapy, and tutoring.

Small changes can make a big difference in the ability of teens with LD or ADHD to perform at their best. Having the student sit in the front of the classroom, adjusting homework assignments, providing tests orally, allowing reading with audio books, offering organizational support, and increasing test-taking time are just a few common changes that schools can make to serve a student's learning needs.

Here's some good news. We now understand that we can significantly improve how our brains work. For example, if a teen has difficulty managing the ability to focus, practice can make a significant difference. There are many tools and techniques for addressing the issues of LD and ADHD. So if your child or teen has ADHD and/or LD, know that with educational therapy and practice, new neural connections can be made and performance improved.

What About the Beast?

If it turns out that your teen does have LD or ADHD, you can use this new information to end the control battle and help your son or daughter move forward toward educational and life success. You'll do this by using all of your skills for ending the parent-teen control battle: holding a healthy vision of your teen, staying positive in tone, and being clear that privileges must be earned. And treatment for LD or ADHD will be part of the program.

Keep in mind, a diagnosis of LD or ADHD is not an excuse; it's an opportunity to take this information and use it as a guide to success. Here is a three-phase approach to help teenagers with LD and ADHD move from frustration and underperformance to independence and success. And even if you don't utilize these phases in a formal way, understanding them can help guide you along this journey.

Phase One: Support

After a teen is assessed and found to have ADHD or LD, it is important that he receive maximum educational and emotional support that takes these issues into account. The goal is to make sure that the teen experiences some initial educational and personal success and is esteemed and given recognition for this. We want him to have that "I *knew* I was smart, and now it's official!" awareness and to feel understood, supported, and optimistic. The message we want him to receive from the results of the assessment is: "You are a lot smarter and more capable than your work has been showing until now. That's because your LD or ADHD has been making it more difficult for your potential to show. With support and accommodations, you will do great."

After discovering a learning disability or ADHD, we want to get as much information about the specific condition as possible. Depending on the level of cooperation your teen demonstrates, include him in choosing the appropriate resources for support.

The questions to stay focused on are: *What are my teen's needs, and what resources are required to meet those needs?* Resources might include tutoring, borrowing class notes, a study skills class or consultant, organizational support, specific software, educational therapy, and careful monitoring by the school counselor. Use those resources very heavily! In this first phase, you want your teenager to begin to love learning, because success is very motivating. In fact, current research indicates that belief in one's ability to be successful is the most significant factor in achieving success for teens, and that includes teens with LD and ADHD (Dweck 2007). When they are motivated, they try, and when they try, with the right support and appropriate expectations, they succeed. Now instead of fighting each other, parents and teen are working together to help teens achieve.

But the novelty of this approach, even with some initial success, can wear off. Now it's time for phase two.

Phase Two: Perseverance

The goal of this phase is to make the initial positive changes permanent. The objective here is for the teen to learn to persevere, and to get past any obstacles. In this phase, teens learn to internalize an attitude of taking responsibility, a critical milestone in their development. What makes this so important is that often these kids have given up on trying hard, and they've been less mature about accepting responsibility.

The danger at this stage is that instead of becoming more capable and responsible, your teen will revert back to acting younger. Seeing this, parents may feel frustrated and defeated, and the Beast will gain new life.

This makes phase two a critical time for parents. When your teenager starts to regress, and old behaviors surface, this is your opportunity to lead your teen to a new level of maturity. Remember, because of their unique struggles to succeed, teens with LD and ADHD often have not learned to be as responsible as they need to be, so it's easy for parents to see them as young and immature. Therefore, it is important to shift your vision and think of your teenager not as being young and irresponsible but as being motivated and capable. By creating and holding this new and healthy vision, and communicating it to your teen, you will naturally maintain accountability to high standards, and your teenager will respond in kind.

Phase Three: Taking Control

This final phase occurs when teens take on full control of their responsibilities and independently use and manage the support system. They know what they need from teachers, parents, counselors, tutors, or other consultants and will contact these individuals on their own. Often this includes regular reviews of progress with a school counselor or educational consultant who acts as a touchstone for the teens. But bear in mind, it's unrealistic to expect kids with LD or ADHD to fully operate in phase three before they are at least sixteen years old.

Let's look at how Luanne and her parents went through these stages.

Luanne

Luanne's father called me for a counseling appointment, saying that his daughter, a fifteen-year-old high school sophomore, had become totally uncooperative, her studies were going downhill, and he and Luanne's mother were at their wits' end with her.

I met with Luanne and her parents, Bob and Lynn. I learned that Luanne had been a good student through elementary school, but in junior high school her excellent grades dropped to B's and C's. Her parents struggled with her through freshman year, trying to get her to do her homework, get to school on time, and manage chores.

When I met Luanne, she was getting C's, D's, and even an occasional F on her schoolwork. She had always enjoyed choir and was still active in it, but now Luanne was in danger of not being allowed to go to a choir competition in another state because of a school policy that restricted students with failing grades from participating. Bob and Lynn were "fed up and burned out." They felt like they were involved in a losing battle. At this point, they were struggling with Luanne about everything—cleaning her room, eating right, getting home on time, and getting off the phone. They were exhausted and the situation was not improving.

Despite their best efforts, Luanne was failing. Now what?

Luanne presented as very bright and personable. She made good eye contact with me and talked as if she had it all together. She reported having many good friends and being involved in lots of activities. Luanne seemed to be far less upset about her grades than her parents were. She said she wasn't worried because she wanted to go to the local community college after high school and was sure she could get in. She felt she could get the F up to a passing grade in her world civilization class once she turned in the rough draft of a major research project. She also said that her parents always wanted her to do better in school than she was able to do.

Luanne and her parents agreed that before the fifth grade, she had caught on quickly, and her bright, involved personality brought her lots of attention and praise from her teachers. But since then, it had become a struggle for her to stay organized, keep track of what was expected, and actually do the work. Luanne said she felt stuck in her schoolwork, which she found overwhelming. It was neither fun nor interesting, and she rarely got good results, so she procrastinated. She would put off her schoolwork until the best she could do with the remaining time would be a substandard or incomplete job.

Bob and Lynn believed that Luanne could do well if she put her mind to it because in classes that she liked, she got A's. They felt that she was too social and that her problems were just the result of her immaturity—thinking that you can get by in life doing only what you want. How could they get Luanne to see this and take her responsibilities seriously?

I agreed with Bob and Lynn that Luanne needed to take her work seriously and become successful in her classes. Getting low grades is not a formula for success. Even if Luanne could be admitted to community college, how would she succeed once she got in? The habit of not trying one's hardest could become a serious character issue.

I helped Bob, Lynn, and Luanne to understand and see the control battle that now defined their relationship, and the serious toll it was taking on all of them. The parents were chronically upset with Luanne and frustrated by her resistance. Luanne had become used to her parents' disapproval and had tuned them out. She lowered her expectations for herself and relegated her parents' criticism to background noise. Sadly, Luanne now thought of herself as not very smart or successful, and she felt like the "problem" in her family.

When we looked at the situation, it made no sense. Luanne was a terrific kid with caring parents, yet they were all feeling pretty miserable. We decided that the Control Battle Beast must be involved and we resolved to defeat it.

I shared with all three of them that Luanne had some very strong red flags for ADHD and learning disabilities. After all, she had excellent verbal skills, was clearly bright and engaged, and in spite of her struggles at school and at home, she was a good person who wanted to please.

Bob and Lynn said that they had thought Luanne might have ADHD, but they didn't want to pursue it because they didn't want her on medication. They felt that if she really wanted to do well, she could, and that she would be better off not using drugs. Luanne, too, had thought she might have ADHD. She had friends who "had it" and were on medication, and they described the same things going on with them. Her friends told her that the medication did help some, but it really didn't seem to change things much.

I explained that medication wasn't the only possible response to ADHD, and there are many ways to help people and teach them to help themselves. I also explained that I was suspicious that Luanne might have learning disabilities as well. We agreed to ask the school to do educational testing, and I would do a screening for ADHD.

My screening revealed that Luanne had enough symptoms to place her in the moderate range of ADHD. While she did not show any hyperactivity, she scored high in distractibility and impulsivity. School testing revealed a significant gap between Luanne's intellectual capability and her performance ability. In other words, she knew more than she could express. The school psychologist explained that distractibility caused by ADHD, auditory processing problems (difficulty understanding verbal instructions), and a reading disorder contributed to her learning challenges.

The school called a meeting with Luanne, her teachers, her parents, the school psychologist, the school counselor, the assistant principal, and me to determine Luanne's eligibility for services and to create an individualized educational plan, or IEP.

After reviewing the testing, the team determined that Luanne was eligible for special education services and decided on a number of accommodations and support elements. These included extended time for test taking, listening to audio recordings of reading assignments, regular assignment reviews and meetings with teachers, close email contact between Luanne's parents and teachers, and meetings twice weekly with a reading specialist, who would teach reading techniques and organizational skills.

We agreed to hold off on any decision to pursue medication for ADHD until we saw how everything else was working. The school psychologist advised Luanne and her parents that Luanne should set her graduation sights higher and plan to go to a four-year college.

Luanne and her parents were amazed and emotionally buoyed by what they'd learned and the support they were given. They all became optimistic for the first time in years.

During this first phase, things improved considerably. Luanne thrived on the attention and support. She was catching up on her school assignments and getting good feedback from her teachers. In fact, everyone started to think that the problems were solved.

After about eight weeks, however, some old patterns began to reemerge. Although Luanne thoroughly enjoyed the support, success, and positive feedback she was receiving, she became less willing to invest the time and energy necessary to maintain it. The old pattern of her parents pushing her to do her work and her chores, and Luanne acting annoyed and resisting, began to return.

I explained to them all that this was only a sign that they were entering phase two, and that I had every confidence that we could move things successfully forward. In family counseling, I taught Bob and Lynn to stay positive and to tie Luanne's cell phone use, Internet access, and social time to conscientiousness and a respectful, cooperative attitude. I taught and coached Luanne to use a respectful tone of voice and body language with her parents. I explained to her how ADHD causes procrastination and distraction. We reviewed several techniques for managing these problems and developed an action plan.

Over the course of the next month, the situation began to show real improvement. Luanne learned that her parents responded well to respectful communication and that they were simply not going to fight with her anymore. Bob and Lynn had established the standards for privileges and it was up to Luanne to earn them if she wanted them.

Phase two was successfully underway. Luanne became more accustomed to staying on top of her responsibilities. The constant arguing at home evaporated, and Luanne was on her way to a more promising future. Once she developed a workable routine for managing her responsibilities, she realized that she still had time for texting, talking, and hanging out with friends. The climate at home had changed from Bob and Lynn fighting with Luanne and trying to force her to take care of her responsibilities to Bob and Lynn supporting Luanne in managing her own responsibilities. Bob and Lynn gave enormous credit and praise to Luanne for the changes she made. They talked with her in a tone that conveyed respect for her as a young adult.

In the summer months, Luanne worked with an educational consultant to develop her reading and writing skills and review prospective colleges. On her own, Luanne talked with her teachers and set the expectations of the grades she wanted to earn. She let them know of her special needs and requested frequent feedback on her progress and status. With phase three underway, Bob and Lynn supported Luanne in getting her driver's license, and she "adopted" her mother's old car. By the beginning of her junior year, Luanne was off and running.

Don't Let the Beast Feed off LD and ADHD

If you are using your best parenting skills to end a control battle, yet your teen continues to struggle with getting schoolwork done or staying on track with responsibilities, a learning disability or ADHD may be part of the problem. Get the best assessments and information you can, and build a team that includes you, the professionals, and your teen. Then use all the tools for ending the control battle to support your teen in believing in herself, using her resources, and creating her own success.

CHAPTER 10

When Parents Don't Agree

Being in a control battle with our teen can be a profoundly frustrating experience. And when the other parent operates very differently from how we do, or seems to actively undermine our best efforts, our feelings of frustration and helplessness can go off the charts. This is the expanded Control Battle.

The *other parent* can take many forms. This person can be the biological parent we're married to, were never married to, or have become divorced from. The other parent can be a stepparent, a grandparent, or any other adult figure who plays a significant parenting role.

If there is unaddressed and unresolved discord between parents, they will quite often blame each other for the teen's problem behaviors. Very commonly, the stricter parent will blame the more flexible parent for undermining him or her and giving the teen opportunities to make mistakes and get in trouble. "What's the point of having rules if everything is an exception?" laments the stricter parent. The more flexible parent sees the problem with the teen's behavior as caused by the other parent's harsh and inflexible approach and offers, "If she sees us as more understanding and flexible, she'll appreciate it and be motivated to behave better!"

Parental Control Battles

While the struggle between a "tougher" and a "softer" parent is by far the most common pattern of parental control battle, other parental relationship patterns can be control battle based too. Sometimes both parents compete to be the more understanding parent. Parents who are not getting their important emotional needs met by each other or another adult will compete for the affections of the teenager and avoid acknowledging and resolving the discord between the adults. This puts the teenager in the untenable position of siding with or pleasing either one parent or the other. Children and teenagers in this position will demonstrate symptoms and problems of many varieties.

In another form of the parental control battle, both parents are tough on their teenager, who provides them with a convenient displacement of an unacknowledged emotional conflict. The one thing the parents agree on is how difficult their son or daughter is, and they constantly focus on what the teen is doing wrong. You can imagine how painful that can be for the teenager who feels that he or she just can't win. Not surprisingly, in turn, teens in this situation offer lots of opportunity for criticism.

These less common forms of parental control battles are more difficult to resolve because the parents aren't acknowledging the personal struggle between them. So if you suspect that these dynamics may be taking place in your family, seeking out the services of an experienced family therapist will be paramount.

Parenting Differently Is the Norm

It's important to know that all parents *do* parent differently from one another. One parent might be a little more aware of and responsive to the kids' feelings, and the other might be better at arranging and doing activities. One parent might be stricter with the rules and day-to-day operations than the other. One could be a good homework resource and school advocate, the other less so. One parent could be more nurturing and the other more challenging. One parent can simply be more available and therefore take a lead role in the parenting approach. These differences are very common and do not need to create parental discord or a parental control battle. In fact, these differences can broaden the range of parental resources available to our kids.

But when parents polarize and the differences between them becomes a source of contention, then we have an expanded control battle that will invariably impact everyone in the family. Sometimes the discord is obvious, with loud voices and fighting. Sometimes it is subtler, with silence or disapproving looks, yet no less acutely felt by the kids.

Pulling Together to End the Parent-Teen Control Battle

Using the ending the parent-teen control battle approach is one way for parents to pull together and stop blaming each other for their teen's behavior. We saw this in chapter 6 with Geoff and Will's parents. In that example, the approach brought the stricter and more flexible parents together to starve the Beast and create a healthy structure for their teen boys.

Yet sometimes parents are so entrenched with their negative views of each other that they are simply not ready to work together on any approach, leaving a fat and happy Beast (the Control Battle) in place. In this case, the more motivated or aware parent will need to take steps and make a difference without the other. And *one parent can make a big difference.*

Here is why the last scenario can work. A family is a small social ecosystem, and like other ecosystems, a significant change in one part of the system will affect other parts of the system. So, if things are that simple, why don't we just make a shift and solve the problem? Well, it's because it's hard to believe that *we* should change *our* parenting behavior; after all, if we see the other parent as causing the problem, why would *we* change *our* approach?

I have to be kinder and more understanding with our son, you might think to yourself. *Someone has to make him feel cared about.* Or, *That kid is so spoiled, someone has to hold the line!*

The strict parent believes that rules and respect are primary and that a strong and unyielding approach is necessary to garner obedience. The more flexible parent believes that understanding and support are critical to kids, and if the approach is too strict, they will feel unloved. So neither parent takes the initiative to change, and that maintains the status quo—the expanded parental control battle.

It is just so much easier for us to see how relatively small changes with the *other* parent could have a big impact. It's hard to see that a change in our own approach can have a big impact as well. Because we are stuck in a control battle, our ability to think out of the control battle paradigm is limited. We tend to think in black and white terms—it's either my way or their way.

Yet if we begin to apply ending the control battle thinking and behavior to the other parent as well as to our teen, we're certain to make progress. And here's how we can do just that.

Ending the Parent-Parent Control Battle

For starters, you need to realize that you are in a control battle with the other parent and that the two of you are stuck in a pattern of behavior that needs to change. You might say to yourself, *In order to help our teenager, I need to end my control battle, end my fight with the other parent. I want to starve the Beast in this situation as well.*

To do this, you will need to use all of your skills for ending the control battle.

- Not being *reactive* is an important first step. You'll want to take your time, be thoughtful in your approach, and not take things personally.

- You will not be *other-person focused*. Instead you will focus on your own responses to the other parent, not on changing the other parent's behavior. You'll trust *him or her* to do that.

- You will use positive words and a *positive tone* with all your family members, even when you feel strongly about something. You will want to offer validation of the other parent's ideas and feelings.

- And, you will want to have a *healthy vision* of your parenting partner as well as of your teen. This is sometimes very difficult when you have a challenging personal relationship that extends beyond the parenting relationship. Yet it is vital.

You're obviously not going to withhold privileges from the other parent, so we'll leave that part out and have faith that when we are being a healthy co-parent, the other parent will come around and be one too.

Aaron

Let's meet Aaron and his parents, Mary and Jack. Fifteen-year-old Aaron is disrespectful toward his parents and is not managing his responsibilities. Early in his sophomore year, Aaron's high school counselor, seeing that Aaron was off to a poor start, suggested counseling for him. When Mom called to make an appointment, I scheduled a time for Aaron and his parents to come in together.

After getting to know them a bit, I learned that Aaron likes to skateboard, plays a little guitar, and wants to work in construction. Mom is a medical technician at the local hospital, and Dad is a sheet metal worker who has been with a large industrial heating and cooling company for several years. Aaron has an older brother who shares a house with friends and works in the produce department of a local supermarket. He also takes classes in graphic design, a field in which he'd eventually like to work.

When I asked about the problem, I learned from both parents that Aaron has not been applying himself in school and has become involved with marijuana and alcohol. They stated that Aaron cannot be counted on to be where he's supposed to be or to do what he's supposed to do.

Mom explained that she is very worried about Aaron's relationship with his Dad. They had always been close, and Aaron liked spending time with his father, doing lots of activities and projects together. Now it seems they can't get along at all. Aaron doesn't listen to his father, and Dad has become extremely critical of everything Aaron does.

Mom wishes that Dad would be more positive with Aaron and do more things with him like they used to. She has some good talks with Aaron, and a pretty good relationship, but feels that he really needs a good relationship with his Dad. She thinks that would make a big difference.

Dad is pretty fed up with Aaron's behavior. He explained that his wife undermines him when he sets limits and she lets Aaron get away with too much. His view is that Aaron manipulates his mother, who can be sweet-talked into anything.

Aaron presented his view that his father has to have everything his way. He explained that he doesn't like school much and wants to go into construction, so doing a bunch of homework in history and English isn't important. He admitted that he does smoke "weed" a bit, but says everyone does and it's "no big deal."

Let's listen in on the conversation in the counseling office.

Neil: So, Aaron, I think it's pretty common for kids to not see how their schoolwork relates to them or the future. And it's also pretty common for kids these days to think that smoking marijuana isn't a big deal. So I'm not surprised to hear that you feel that way. But you're fifteen years old. You're not supposed to understand everything yet. That's why you have parents. Both your mother and your father want you to take your schoolwork seriously, and they're both concerned about your marijuana and alcohol use. Why is it that you trust your judgment over theirs? After all, they're pretty experienced people who want what's best for you.

Aaron: Because it doesn't really matter what I do, I'm still gonna get yelled at and told I'm lazy. So what's the point?

Neil: Well, that does sound rather unpleasant. Is that why you've stopped trying in school?

Aaron: Yeah. My teachers don't like me, and I just want to be with my friends. What's wrong with that?

Neil: So it feels like all the grownups are against you. Is that right?

Aaron: Not my mom. But I just like being with my friends, that's all.

Neil: So, Mom and Dad, it seems that Aaron is pretty closed off from his education and I can see where it's pretty tough to get cooperation from him. His motivation and his trust are pretty low. I can see what you're struggling with.

Mom: It is a struggle and I feel bad for him. I just think if he had a better relationship with his dad, he'd listen to him. I tell him his dad loves him, but he's not that interested in what I've got to say.

Dad: I think you're getting the idea here, Neil; everything is my fault. It's my fault that he smokes pot, doesn't do his schoolwork, and is disrespectful to me and his mother. If I point out anything he needs to do, I'm "picking on him." If he does a crappy job and I point it out, I'm "being mean." I'm supposed to have a good relationship with Aaron. I ask him for help on a project and he says "sure," and then he doesn't show up. When I get upset, his mother tells me that's the way teenagers are. I'm just old fashioned. It's okay these days for kids to do what they want and be disrespectful.

Neil: Yikes, Dad! You're pretty pissed off about things. And I can understand that you feel like you can't get anywhere with your son, that he's at risk of going downhill, and that you can't get support for dealing with it from you wife. That would be extremely frustrating.

Dad: I'm used to it at this point, Neil. I don't see anything I can do. Maybe you can meet with Aaron and talk sense into him. I sure can't.

Neil: Actually, Dad, I don't think I would be any more successful than you. So let me tell you what I'm noticing and what I'm thinking. In fact let me tell *all* of you and then let me hear from you all what you think about my ideas. Because I need to be sure that I understand the problem correctly if I'm going to be helpful to you. And if we are all on the same page and we all understand the problem, then we can all work together to fix it. Make sense? (I receive a nod of acknowledgment from all three, and proceed.)

First of all, I'm with a terrific family. A family where there is a lot of caring, two hardworking parents, and, up until recently, some pretty good success at raising kids. Aaron is a neat kid with a good idea for his future, and he enjoys skateboarding and playing guitar. Your older son is doing quite well, but we're at a stuck point with your second son, now in the middle of his teenage years. I'm glad you're here because it does seem that we're at a crossroads for Aaron. Either he and his parents are going to pull together so he can go forward in a healthy way, or we'll see him struggle, make some serious mistakes, and the whole family will end up being pretty miserable.

At this point, it feels to me very much like the three of you are all tied up in a knot. That everyone feels like they can't be effective, can't be successful with each other. Aaron, it feels to you like you can't get any support or be successful at home or at school, no matter what you do. Mom, it feels like you can't be successful with Aaron or with his Dad, that you're blocked by both of them. Unless they get together, there's nothing you can do. Dad, you're feeling like you can't be successful with Aaron because he hides behind Mom and she blames you for his behavior. No matter what you do, you're blocked. To me this feels like one big knot.

Dad: That's pretty much it in a nutshell, Neil.

Mom: (Nodding in agreement)

Neil: What about you Aaron, what do you think?

Aaron: Sure.

I explained how the parent-teen control battle works and how it was operating in their family.

Neil: And in your family there is an extra complication: there is a mother-father control battle as well. If we really want to get things back on track, we're going to need to end both control battles, because at this point we've got one big happy Beast, and three unhappy family members. And that's not acceptable.

I made an individual appointment with Aaron to gain a deeper understanding of him and his issues and made an appointment with Mom and Dad without Aaron as well.

Here's part of my conversation with Dad and Mom.

Jack: I can tell you right now, Neil, this is going to be the "change Jack hour." I've been to counseling before and the counselor and Mary decided that I'm the one who needs to change, and I'm telling you, no matter what I do, it will never be good enough.

Neil: That is indeed a lousy way to feel, Jack, but I'm not looking to blame anyone. In fact, let's leave the whole idea of blame outside. I'm interested in starving the Beast and helping you and Mary end your control battle, which is undermining your ability to effectively raise Aaron, and I'm guessing that it's taking a big toll on your personal relationship as well.

Jack: That's for sure. We used to go to shows, enjoy our friends together, watch sports. Now all Mary does is fret about Aaron and talk with her friends. And I'm the bad guy. It's actually been going on for a few years now.

Mary: It's hard to get close to someone who is so negative and critical all the time. I want to be close to Jack, but I want him to be nice to Aaron and to me, too. He's just always so negative.

I asked them both if they'd be willing to try an experiment and let me coach them in a new kind of communication, one that could make a real difference in their relationship. They agreed, and I showed Jack and Mary how to use the validation tool with each other.

They tried it, and they were both amazed at how dramatically it changed the feeling between them. Mary reported that it was the first time in years that she experienced that warm, safe place with Jack that she had loved so much about him when they'd first met. Jack said it was good to get something more positive from Mary and to feel like he wasn't the bad guy for a change.

Now that the feeling in the room was more positive and was emotionally safer, we were able to uncover that Mary grew up with a scary alcoholic father, and Jack's criticism and anger triggered her old feelings. This pushed her away and made her protective of Aaron. We learned that Jack grew up pretty much on his own, with no father and a working beleaguered mother; he had been looked after mostly by his brothers. He had to learn to fend for himself and can't understand why Aaron is so irresponsible and ungrateful.

I helped Jack and Mary understand why these issues made for such fertile ground for the control battle. I showed each of them how they could make a dramatic shift whenever the control battle started. By offering validation, it would immediately shift the feeling between them. I helped Jack see that he was never as stuck as he thought he was. Even though he did need to be cautious about being critical, that did not mean everything was his fault. It simply meant that he had the opportunity to either feed or starve the Beast. I showed Mary that even though she was easily triggered, she could recognize the difference between her father and Jack, and that she too had the opportunity to starve or feed the Beast.

Over the next couple of meetings, Mary and Jack practiced applying the plan for ending the control battle, which involved

- avoiding being reactive (this was tough for both of them, but they both improved considerably),

- focusing their efforts solely on their own behaviors, and not being other-person focused, and

- practicing their validation skills, which helped them stay positive in their tone.

I helped them to understand that they are not likely to use their best skills at the same time, but if either one of them stepped up and did use their best skills, it would shift things out of the control battle. Either one of them could be the leader at any time.

After making some headway with ending the parental control battle, we convened a family session to have The

Talk. Aaron was actually quite open to the new family order even though he now had higher standards to live up to. He had noticed the change in tone at home and had softened up as a result. He was not nearly as resolute against school and authority.

There was to be regular study time every Monday through Thursday and weekends, and weekly testing for THC, the active ingredient in marijuana. Back talk and badgering would no longer be accepted. Privileges included opportunities to go out with his friends and use of his skateboard, phone, and video games.

We worked together for a number of months, and during this time Mary came to understand that she's not responsible for other people's happiness or for Jack and Aaron's relationship. This turned out to make her much happier.

Jack began to realize that his negative views of Mary and Aaron were his enemies, not Mary and Aaron. He came to realize that they each needed him and that he didn't need to take adolescent behavior so personally. He learned more about Mary's "triggers" and was more understanding, sympathetic, and supportive to her.

From the sessions, Aaron learned that he had a lot more influence over ending the control battle—and therefore over his life —than he had realized. Not surprisingly, when Aaron started doing his work, he became much more successful in school and reported that he actually felt a lot better off marijuana. He still wished that he could smoke it from time to time, but he knew he'd lose his privileges if he did. Aaron thought that after high school he might take courses in construction at the local community college and then take construction management at a four-year state college. This sense of purpose and opportunity was very motivating to him. Aaron and his father built a skateboard half-pipe in the backyard, and Aaron and his friends loved it. Occasionally, Jack would drive Aaron and his friends to a nearby town with a skateboard park and they'd make a day of it.

So if you want to end your control battle with your teenager and you're feeling defeated by the other parent, you are not stuck. You can still end it. But because this can be quite complex, and because there are often underlying issues that create the fertile ground for these dynamics, counseling should be given strong consideration. That way you will be in a safe environment to uncover the critical issues, shift out of the polarized positions, and begin to work together. With or without counseling, remember that if you avoid being reactive or other-person focused, use a positive tone, keep a healthy vision of your teen, your partner, and yourself, and let your teen be in charge of earning his privileges, you *can* starve the Beast.

CHAPTER 11

When Your Teen Is Seriously Out of Control

Teens who are out of control, at serious risk, and unresponsive to parental requirements are referred to by mental health professionals as "beyond parental control," or BPC. As we have established in this book, parents don't actually control their teens; parents can only control their own parenting. Teens control their own behavior. So it would be more accurate to refer to this group as "teens who are not managing their behavior appropriately, are not accountable to parental authority, and are now seriously at risk." But that would be a bit cumbersome, so for the sake of terminology, let's just refer to this group with the common term, BPC.

BPC teenagers

- **Have an extreme lack of accountability to parents.** They operate largely outside of parental structures, rules, and expectations. BPC teens may stay out all night, lie about where they are, and not return calls or texts.

- **Almost always abuse drugs.** They often use daily, or several times daily. In addition to marijuana and alcohol, some BPC teens use higher-risk drugs such as methamphetamine, cocaine, heroin, prescription painkillers, and psychedelics. They may also be selling drugs.

- **Are often sexually active and sexually unsafe.** They may not appropriately protect against sexually transmitted diseases or pregnancy, may have multiple partners, and may put themselves in unsafe situations where they can become victims—or even perpetrators—of sexual violence.

- **Have in large part discontinued their relationships with healthy peers.** BPC teens tend to hang out only with other kids who support their destructive behavior pattern. They have withdrawn from their healthy personal and social activities such as team sports, music, art, or performing arts programs.

- **May become involved with the juvenile justice system.** Sometimes they're involved in a minor way, such as being cited for possession of a small amount of alcohol or drugs, or a curfew violation. And sometimes they are arrested for more serious violations, such as shoplifting, vandalism, selling drugs, or acts of violence.

- **Often have thoughts of, make threats of, or attempt suicide.** They often suffer from depression and may be self-cutting or exhibiting other self-destructive behaviors.

- **Are extremely difficult to communicate with.** They may be aggressively defensive in any discussion, or simply lie and agree to anything you say, and then do what they want.

As we discussed in chapter 1, control battles can interfere with adolescent development. Teens who are BPC are often lacking in their values development. They have little respect for authority, have not developed a sense of personal responsibility, ignore or try to get around the rules, and are often dishonest.

How Does a Teen's Behavior Get This Destructive?

Family dynamics of this nature don't pop up overnight. Teens who are BPC have typically been in a control battle with their parents or guardians for an extended period of time, long enough for the relationship pattern to become seriously entrenched.

Trauma or a serious disruption in a teen's life may have encouraged the negative behavior. Or, the teen may have been involved with substance abuse or destructive behaviors without the parent's awareness, and when this abuse is discovered, the break in connection and trust between the family members creates a control battle that gets to the BPC stage very quickly.

My Teen Is BPC! Now What?

If your teen is this far out of control, unaccountable, and shows any signs of high-risk behavior, there is urgent need of a major intervention. Going along and hoping that things will get better can result in a life-changing crisis. Profound life-altering outcomes can include significant injury or death, drug overdose or alcohol toxicity, suicide, becoming the victim of sexual assault, or arrest and incarceration for a significant crime with major legal consequences. Other serious outcomes can include school failure or expulsion, drug dependence, and simply developing a negative identity and impaired social and emotional development.

Barriers to Taking Action

Parents in these situations sometimes feel blackmailed by their son or daughter, who may have shown them—through words or actions—that if they try to set limits, they will make things even worse. Parents will often rationalize their lack of response to the crisis in these ways:

- At least he's going to school most of the time. If I ground him, he'll just take off and I won't know where he is at all.

- If I confront him about his behavior, he'll just explode and walk out. I don't want to put the whole family through that.

- If I take his phone away, I'll lose all contact with him.

- At least he's not using hard drugs. I smoked pot when I was a teenager.

- She's told me that the only thing that matters to her is her friends. If I try to restrict her, she says she'll run away. And then anything could happen to her!

- If I come down on him, he'll think both his parents are against him.

In this way, parents are attempting to control their teen through inaction, but this inaction only supports the control battle and their teen's self-destructive behavior. There may be other control battle–based behaviors that the parents and teen engage in that support the BPC behavior; they might fight, yell, accuse, and threaten, all of which are simply ways to engage each other that maintain the status quo of the parent-teen control battle–based relationship.

Can This Still Be Turned Around? When Is It Too Late?

When things get this bad, it's quite common for parents to lose all hope that things will ever get better, that their teen will ever be healthy. And this lack of hope and healthy vision will only empower the Beast. But when teens are this far out of control, is it reasonable to think that things *can* get better? Is there any hope? Is there anything we can do? In other words, if we do things differently, will we get a different response from our kid? If we operate outside of the control battle, will things change?

The answer is yes —they will and they must. If you take the critical steps to starve the Beast and end the control battle, you can change the direction in which this is headed. It may not be quick and it may not be easy, but if you commit to ending your participation in the control battle and take healthy action, things will turn around.

What Resources Will It Take to Accomplish This?

In order for you to learn what your teen needs and exactly what actions to take, you will need to make critical changes and observe the results. You will then see how your teenager responds, which will help you determine what additional steps to take. As in other situations requiring a restart, you'll begin with The Talk.

- Make it clear that you love and have faith in your teen, and enumerate his or her many strengths.

- Clarify that what is going on is unacceptable and be absolutely clear about the behaviors that need to change.

- Apologize for participating in the control battle and allowing things to get this far without taking stronger action.

- Clarify your specific expectations going forward, including the privileges that must be earned and are being withdrawn.

- If your teen needs help succeeding with any of your expectations, including school, or is dealing with emotional issues such as depression, or with substance abuse, offer to help find appropriate resources such as tutoring or counseling. In fact, utilizing these resources may well be a requirement.

Many BPC teenagers have become so unaccountable that they won't sit still to listen to you and will simply rage or walk out. In this case, you can write all this down and hand it to your teen or leave it where he will see it, or even text it if that is your only option. In fact, writing the outline of your talk and giving it to your teen is a good idea anyway because it makes it clearer, more tangible, and real, and it creates a document you can refer back to.

Be aware that when you write down your expectations, it is not a contract (if she does X, she gets Y). Contracts are generally agreements between equal parties, and the implementation of a contract can be disputed. You are simply writing down your expectations and clarifying your teen's privileges. Remember to include how terrific your teen is and to enumerate his strengths. We don't want our written communication to support the control battle any more than our verbal communication does.

Making the Shift

It's important to not have expectations that The Talk will have a direct effect on your teen's behavior, particularly since the negative behavior is so extreme. When your teen continues with the unacceptable behavior, simply observe and take note, repeat your expectations, and see what happens. You will need to take some immediate action to be true to your word that privileges will be withdrawn unless earned, such as discontinuing cell phone or computer access, use of vehicles, and money. Once again, this is not designed to coerce your youth into changing—that would simply be a new strategy within the control battle. Instead, what you're doing is starving the Control Battle Beast by staying positive and following a simple, healthy parenting guideline: privileges are offered only when they're earned.

Success Is in the Details

Now that you have established the expectations and are communicating positively and outside of the control battle, you will need to take action in many aspects of your teen's life. This can include requiring your teen to build a closer, more engaged connection to school, such as by meeting with teachers and making a plan to get caught up on work or by joining a sports team. It might mean helping your teen to find a new, more appropriate school setting; requiring and monitoring positive social and recreational activity; getting appropriate educational, psychological, and/or psychiatric assessments, including substance abuse screening; obtaining family and individual counseling and substance abuse treatment; requiring employment if appropriate; and requiring your teen to spend more time with other (healthy) family members and to be more involved in family activities such as cooking, cleaning, and recreation. It could also mean involving family friends, relatives, and neighbors for engagement and support, and possibly even involving law enforcement and juvenile probation to support your parental authority.

What Are the Goals of This Effort?

There are essentially three goals for this approach:

1. teen accountability to parental authority,

2. clean and sober behavior, and

3. positive educational and social engagement.

Your efforts will take time and persistence to be effective. Remember, BPC youth have fallen behind in their social and emotional development, so their values, including honesty and trustworthiness, will take time to develop. There will be problem behaviors along the way. These problems and relapses—returning to old negative behaviors—need to be treated as learning opportunities for your teen and must be dealt with outside of the control battle. As long as you stay positive and require that privileges be earned, your teenager will continue to learn, grow, and develop.

When Should Parents Consider Residential Placement?

Residential treatment is an excellent and often necessary option for parents of BPC teens. Residential programs immediately remove kids from negative peer and community influences and cut off access to their destructive behaviors. The programs build self-esteem, responsibility, and accountability and provide a plan for overall personal success. Generally, kids end up loving their residential programs and form close relationships with the staff.

A residential program can be considered anytime. And even if it's never used, investigating and knowing that those resources are there can help parents feel confident that no matter what, they have a way to help their teen get under control and be safe.

Some parents may discover that they simply don't have the resources to give their BPC teen the structure and support that's needed at home and in the community. Parents may be emotionally burned out or simply have demanding jobs with no other adults available to provide what their teen needs. While working to end the control battle and turn things around, it may become clear that a teen is so involved with drugs, a negative peer culture, and unsafe behavior that a residential program is the only safe option.

There are a wide range of programs for BPC youth, catering to a variety of needs and age groups. The websites for these programs look inviting, but finding the right program for your particular teenager will make all the difference in achieving a successful outcome. Educational placement consultants have significant first-hand experience with the programs. They regularly visit them and know how they work with different kinds of kids. It would be overwhelming to try to make a decision about placement without the support, guidance, and expertise of a qualified educational consultant.

And we want the program—or the consideration of placement—to be part of ending the control battle. If placement is used as a threat, or just another way to control a teen, it will fail. It will feel like control and punishment to a kid. But if it is set up correctly, it can be seen as a way to help a teen become safe and get back on track.

The option of placement in a program should be part of an open discussion between parents and their teenager. When parents are clear that things must and will turn around, they can simply ask their teenager if he needs the structure and support of a program to be able to change his behavior. Sometimes kids will acknowledge this need even if they don't like the idea. Other times it will help kids understand that things have radically changed and it will motivate them to end their BPC behavior and start cooperating.

Often parents will be quite reluctant to utilize a residential program. They may be concerned that

- their teen will experience it as betrayal, rejection, or abandonment;

- it will expose their teen to other negative teens;

- the programs will be harsh and dangerous; or

- it will be too expensive.

Programs are generally strength-based and use approaches that have been tested and proven to be therapeutic. Programs actively involve parents in their teen's recovery through regular and active therapeutic communication and onsite parent weekends. Placement in a therapeutic program is not rejection or abandonment; it's an investment in a better outcome and shows the true commitment parents have to their teen. If you are considering a placement and are concerned about the cost, speak with an educational placement consultant, who can look into scholarships and insurance reimbursement.

Luke

Let's look at a BPC situation with Luke, age sixteen, and two possible ways to proceed toward resolution. Luke's mother and father had a volatile marriage and divorced about five years ago. Luke lives with his mother and stepfather, and part of the time with his eleven-year-old stepbrother. Luke's father lives about an hour away and after the divorce would see Luke every other weekend, on holidays, and several weeks in the summer. Luke's mother has felt undermined by Luke's father, who thinks she is too strict and would set few limits for him. Luke and his father used to go motocross riding together, and Luke even competed for a year, but their passion for it eventually waned. As Luke got older, he went to his father's house less and less, and their relationship dropped off.

Luke has always resented his mother for being too strict and blames her for the divorce. He's never accepted his mother's new husband, even though his stepfather tried to reach out to Luke. Luke has never been kind toward his stepbrother, Shawn, who looks up to him and seeks his approval.

Luke's mother has alternated between feeling guilty and protective of Luke, and feeling frustrated and angry. She has felt responsible for his situation and has not wanted to come down too hard on him.

More and more, Luke wants only to skateboard and hang out with his skater friends. Up until this year, Luke's mom had been able to keep him more or less on track. When he fell behind in school, she would ground him until he was caught up. Although she knew he sometimes drank and smoked cigarettes and pot, she hoped to keep it from getting out of hand. Whenever he was caught, she grounded him and he usually shaped up for a while. His attitude would improve, and he would even be nicer to Shawn and play video games with him. However, after a while, things would slide back to how they were before, and he would do something else wrong.

Late in the first semester of Luke's junior year, his mother found out that he was failing most of his classes. She had backed off trying to manage Luke's homework schedule because he objected so much and it no longer seemed appropriate, given his age. During our counseling session she explained that, frankly, she was exhausted from the battles day and night.

It turned out that Luke was skipping school and had done few of his assignments, so the school was recommending that he go to an alternative high school for students not able to manage the structure or homework of a mainstream high school. But Luke's mother was against this because she knew he was able to do the work, and she didn't want to give Luke more time to get into trouble. Luke, on the other hand, wanted to go to the alternative school because he had some friends there, could get out of school by noon, and wouldn't have homework. The school recommended counseling to help the family make a decision, but the principal made it clear that he didn't want Luke back unless he was committed to going to all his classes and doing his work.

When I met with Luke and his mother, Luke was clearly unhappy about being there. He made no eye contact with me, responded to my handshake weakly, and moved around with angry gestures. His dress was typical of many "skaters"—baggy pants, a black leather jacket, lots of chains, and a wool cap.

May, Luke's mother, was a pleasant woman and was obviously embarrassed by her son's behavior. She told me that he was not usually like this, but he really didn't want to be there. I told May that it is common for kids to not want to be in counseling, and not to worry about it. Luke replied to my questions with grunts of "I dunno," "fine," "alright," or "I guess so." I acknowledged that he wasn't up for engaging right now and went on to discuss the reason for the visit with May.

Neil: May, what is going on that you would like some help with?

May: The school is ready to kick Luke out. They want him to go to an alternative school and Luke wants to go there, too, but I'm not sure that's the answer.

Neil: What are your concerns?

May: Luke is smart and I know he can do the work. He's just lazy and lately his attitude has gotten worse and worse. He's hanging out with kids who are going nowhere, and Luke is getting to be more and more like them.

Luke: There's nothing wrong with my friends. You and Ron (Luke's stepfather) are just against skaters. You're just siding with Ron against them.

May: I often feel in the middle between Luke and Ron. Luke never accepted my relationship with Ron, even when Ron made an effort to connect with him. Luke thinks all my rules and discipline come from Ron, which isn't true. But he doesn't listen to me.

Luke: Well, it *is* true. If Ron thought the alternative school was a good idea, I'd already be there. He doesn't understand me, and you always follow all his advice, even if it's stupid.

May: At this point it doesn't seem to matter what I say or why I say it, Luke. You come and go as you please and it really doesn't seem to matter to you what the rule is or who's making it. You just do whatever you want.

As the discussion went on, it became quite clear that there was a longstanding control battle raging in this family. Mom felt completely undermined by Luke's absentee father. Her husband, Ron, felt undermined by May and Luke's father, and Luke fought control by Ron and his mother, yet he received no guidance or limits from his father. And while I wasn't sure what Luke's father felt, I was suspicious that he might be using Luke to hurt May. The bottom line at this point was that Luke was not accountable to anyone, was on a path to substance abuse and school failure, and was at risk for many other problems.

This was clearly a BPC situation. With accountability missing from the equation, it was going to be tough to get an initial foothold on some solutions. I explained my concerns to May and Luke: that Luke was a kid without healthy positive activities other than perhaps skateboarding; that he didn't seem to have a direction or goal in life, and that's not a good thing for a sixteen-year-old. I explained that substance abuse is a pattern of behavior that gets worse with time and that Luke was moving in a bad direction. He was certainly not preparing in any reasonable way for a successful future, and without any accountability, he was at risk of getting into trouble. Luke was making very poor decisions for himself and wasn't open to anyone else to guide and help him with that.

I also shared that I thought Luke seemed like a nice kid, certainly a strong-minded kid, but that with all the negativity in his life, the lack of positive adult relationships, and the anger he had been expressing, he very likely could be experiencing depression.

I explained that I didn't see how leaving his high school and going to a school with much lower standards would solve anything—particularly if he didn't attend that school either.

May: What you're saying makes sense. But what am I supposed to do?

Luke: Let's get out of here, Mom. He's just the next idiot you're going to listen to so I can't change schools.

I told May that it was imperative that Luke's father and Ron come to the next session with her. I told her that her son did not appear ready to make any serious changes in his life, and he needed the adults who cared about him and were responsible for him to make some decisions about what to do. I told Luke that I would be happy to meet with him alone so he could tell me more about what was going on with him and give me the chance to better understand him. He didn't look up. I also told Luke that it would be smart to come to the next meeting since some important decisions about his future would be discussed.

Luke's parents and stepfather had some important decisions to make. To do nothing would mean watching Luke go downhill into substance abuse and life failure. Because Luke was underage and they were supporting him, they were in effect supporting his decline.

Let's look at two ways things could work out for Luke.

Scenario One

I set up a phone consultation with Luke's father, Harry. Harry said that he felt that Ron was controlling May and trying to run Luke, too, and he understood Luke's feelings about it. I told Harry that clearly there were some hard feelings and struggles among the adults, but that now that Luke was in trouble, the adults needed to put some of their feelings aside and decide together how to help Luke get back on track. Harry acknowledged that he was worried about Luke, who was smoking a lot of pot, and that he wasn't seeing him much. He agreed to work with May and Ron to help Luke get off of drugs and get back on track. Harry said he was willing to be more involved with Luke.

All the adults and Luke met together. The adults were surprisingly quite civil with each other and focused on the issues with Luke. Luke wasn't happy about it, but he was more cooperative and less rude than during his first visit. Harry, Ron, and May all talked about what a terrific person they know Luke to be and how concerned they were with his pot and alcohol use and his lack of responsibility and direction. Even Luke acknowledged that he knew things needed to change.

A plan was made whereby Harry was going spend a lot more time with Luke. Luke was going to need to demonstrate a positive attitude, be kind to Shawn, and test negative for marijuana before he could have any independent free time.

Shortly after the session, Luke was drug tested and high levels of THC showed up, confirming his parent's concerns about marijuana abuse and justifying their requirement for regular drug tests. The parents required Luke to get a job, with the understanding that they would monitor a plan for saving and spending. Harry helped him make a plan and look for jobs. Eventually Luke got a job with a landscaper who appreciated how fast Luke worked and came to quickly rely on him as an important asset to his business. Luke attended individual and family counseling sessions. He was allowed to attend the alternative school, where he set and was held accountable to appropriate learning goals. After a six-month period, Luke and his parents felt very successful. Luke had developed a significant level of independence and worked steadily. He was saving for a truck and was able to get his driver's license. His stated long-term goal was to own his own landscape business.

In this scenario, when the adults put aside their very complex parental control battle and worked together, Luke was able to accept their authority, be accountable, and become responsible and successful. He was a heck of a lot happier, too.

Scenario Two

After the family meeting, Harry drove up to spend time with Luke a couple of times, but he was unable to act or sound authoritative. Luke had mostly stopped sleeping at home, and instead was staying at his friend's house, where he was able to maintain his self-destructive lifestyle. Luke often came by his mother's house during the day to get clothes and food, and many times small amounts of money would be missing. Luke's mother learned that Luke was dealing marijuana and riding around with his friend, most likely stoned. She was at her wits' end trying to get Luke to come home when he was supposed to.

May started to see residential placement as the only option, so I referred her to an educational placement consultant. Since Luke was not at all cooperative, they arranged to have an escort service take him to a six-week wilderness program.

When he arrived, Luke admitted to using many other drugs and to being depressed, both common issues among teens in the program. Luke did well there as he learned to open up in therapy groups. He thrived with the structure and support. May came to the program's parent weekend, and she and Luke started to build a new honest and healthy relationship.

Despite his progress, it was clear that Luke still lacked the self-control or personal goals to come home and be successful there, so the educational consultant and the wilderness program staff identified an excellent therapeutic boarding school for Luke.

During his nine months at the school, his self-esteem skyrocketed. He excelled in the educational component and began doing advanced work. He loved the wilderness outings and developed impressive naturalist skills and knowledge. He came home with a plan to go to college and get a degree in environmental engineering. He enrolled in the alternative school and took several classes at the local community college. He got a job at the local climbing gym, where he was promoted to instructor and worked as an instructional aide on real rock climbing outings.

The Power of Resolve

In these two scenarios, you can see that once the parents decided they were no longer going to be intimidated by their teen's behavior, they were able to end their participation in the control battle, move forward, and take action. They were able to help their teenager get back on a healthy path to success. Although BPC teen behavior is extremely serious, it can be transformed, but only if we starve the Beast.

Final Thoughts

We've taken a journey together, so let's look back over the ground we've covered and think about how to put the concepts and tools we've learned to best use for the future.

We now understand that the Control Battle is an entity in and of itself we're calling "the Beast." We've learned that the Beast has a powerful impact on our relationship with our teen and that unless we are aware of its presence, and how we unwittingly empower it, it will continue to thrive. And perhaps most importantly, we've learned that we cannot effectively support and guide our teenagers unless we ourselves operate outside of the control battle.

Chapter 2 gave a picture of what adolescence really is and why this time of life is such an invitation to the control battle. By understanding the social, emotional, physical, and neurological changes taking place during adolescence, we can have greater patience and empathy for our teenagers and be less inclined to take their behaviors personally.

I've offered you some surefire ways to end your control battle, but if you merely apply a technique without a clear vision of what you're trying to accomplish, your efforts could end up being pulled into the control battle.

Remember, all ongoing relationships have patterns, and those patterns have a way of enduring, repeating, and becoming so familiar that we continue those patterns without thinking about it. If you are in a control battle with your teen, it means that you and your teen have developed an unhealthy, unproductive relationship pattern. In ending your control battle, you are changing an unhealthy pattern and beginning anew to create a healthy one. When you apply a technique, your intention is to change the way you interact with your teen and therefore the pattern of interaction with your teen.

We're talking about making a real change in your family dynamics, getting off the hamster wheel where you put out lots of effort and go nowhere. What you are creating is very different in its nature from what has been going on: a structural change, a different axis, a different dimension entirely. You're going from "Our kid is going in the wrong direction and there's nothing we can do about it!" to "This is a fabulous kid, let's support him in his fabulousness—and here's how we'll do it."

The new healthy pattern includes not being reactive, using a positive tone, and relinquishing your desire for control of your teen's behavior, instead having faith that your teen will make healthier decisions as you begin to starve the Beast. This healthy pattern also includes having clear, reasonable, and high standards and expectations of what your teen will need to achieve in order to earn privileges.

What we're talking about here is the concept of change. And change involves several elements:

- knowing what you want to change, that is, what behaviors you want to stop,

- knowing the behaviors you want to start or develop, and

- regular conscientious application of the new behaviors.

This is true whether we're talking about starting to exercise, being more organized, eating healthier food, changing your golf swing, or in this case, relating to your teen and responding to your teen's behaviors in a new and promising way. If you apply these three concepts until the new behavior seems natural, you will experience sustainable success.

And this is exactly what I want for you and your teen.

My goal is to help you create a significant change by following a few basic principles. Yet few of us make big changes easily and stick with them. After all, if the changes that I'm suggesting came naturally to you, you would most likely already be doing them.

As you were reading *Ending the Parent-Teen Control Battle*, there were probably ideas, issues, and recommended changes that resonated with you more than others. Perhaps there were parts of the book you felt didn't relate to your situation, and then other parts where you said, "That's me! That's us!"

Of the three ways we create and maintain control battles, think about which ones relate to you the most.

- Are you very reactive? Is there a temperamental difference between you and your teen that makes your relationship particularly challenging?

- Do you tend to be overly helpful and perhaps even "other-person focused?"

- Do you bring a negative tone when setting limits or giving instructions?

Write down the two or three things that are most challenging for you; these will offer the greatest opportunity for you to change the relationship pattern.

You might want to work on being less reactive and clearer about your expectations. You might choose to focus on making more validating statements. Or you might want to communicate more faith in your teen. Perhaps you will choose to work on engaging with your teen more around things that are of interest to her, giving you the opportunity to see and acknowledge the knowledge and skills that she applies in these areas.

Some parents might not be reactive and might use a positive tone and be supportive most of the time, but they may need to focus their change efforts on being clearer and establishing the standards by which privileges are earned. This is all unique and personal to you.

Now that you've thought about this and identified your greatest areas of opportunity to create real change, take an index card and write

1. the behaviors I've identified that feed the Beast,

2. the specific behaviors I will stop, and

3. the new behaviors I will use.

For instance, Ray's parent might write this:

1. I often overreact to what Ray says.

2. I will stop arguing with Ray.

3. When Ray argues, I will listen and warmly let him know that I hear and understand his feelings and his point of view, and repeat my expectation.

And Annie's parent might write this:

1. I am too "other-person focused" with Annie; I keep trying to get her to do her work.

2. I will quit nagging Annie to do her work.

3. When Annie is avoiding her work, I will remind her only one time that we want to support her in having her

privileges, and that she needs to manage her responsibilities to keep them. I will ask her if she needs any help, and then let go.

On another card, make a list of many of your teenager's good qualities, as in these examples:

Ray is a passionate, strong-minded kid. He is loyal, caring, strong, athletic, smart, and multi-talented.

Ray has excellent initiative and a good sense of what he wants.

Ray has great attributes for success in life.

Annie is bright, articulate, creative, funny, caring, lovable, adventuresome, engaging, and capable.

Annie is musically and artistically talented.

Annie is growing and learning and will do great in life.

Keep these two cards with you and refer to them often; making it a habit to refer to them morning, noon, and night will help you stay focused on your goals.

Chapter 6 offered The Talk as a way of creating the fundamental shift you need to end your control battle. If you haven't already implemented The Talk, it's a great way to start things going in the right direction. You can even have a version of The Talk every month or so to review progress and set new goals.

Don't expect yourself to perform your new chosen behaviors perfectly. There will be many situations that seem like gray areas. You'll inevitably make judgments that seem right at the time but might be taken advantage of and not work out. Or you may simply forget what you established and go back to old patterns.

Be kind to yourself. Focus on those things that you are doing well and feel good about them. Perhaps you are not overreacting and you're staying calm, but your teen seems to be taking advantage of the calm and is interpreting it to mean that he can get his way. That's okay; you've gone a step in the right direction. Now you can take the next step. Count the positives and give yourself time to correct the areas that still need focus and improvement.

Not only do you need to be positive and have faith in your teen, you need to be positive and have faith in *yourself*. Remember, no one ever promised your teen a perfect parent, only one that loves the heck out of him and will do her best. Some of you reading this book never even had that.

I want to thank you for spending this time with me; it's given me great pleasure to have this conversation with you. I can't express how gratifying it is to help families end their control battle and in the process bring back their best selves and the ability to once again enjoy their family. I hope this book gives you and your family back your best selves, free of the Beast, and free to be the wonderful people you truly are.

Acknowledgments

I would not and could not have written this book without the support, encouragement, and professional input from many wonderful people.

This journey started with School Superintendent Kathleen Howard, who believed that I had a unique message and asked me to speak with parents at her middle school. It was Kathleen Middleton of Toucan Ed Publishing who encouraged me to put my ideas into a book and helped me get started.

Special thanks to Robin Holland for helping me clarify and "spark my message," and to Diane Tyrell, my editor, for organizing the manuscript and making me sound like a writer. You're my team.

I offer huge thanks to Richard Alloy, Natalie Bitton, Terri Virostko, John Fleming, Mark Burdick, and my cousin Alice Goldin for their expertise and thoughtful input into specific subject areas.

Deep gratitude to my many friends and colleagues who offered material and moral support, including Phyllis and Dick Wasserstrom, Pam and Terry Moriarty, Linda and Bruce Weed, Mary and Marty Golden, Andrea Wachter and Steve Legallet, Susan Karp and Ed Farrar, Carmen and Andy Kumasaka, Suzanne Herrera-Guillory and John Guillory, Timothy Ondahl and Barbara Peterson, and Judy and Jim Schultze.

I'd like to thank the team at New Harbinger Publications for their enthusiasm and valuable feedback, and Rona Bernstein for her incredibly talented editing.

And last but not least I offer my heartfelt thanks to my fabulous wife, Eileen Brown, for her input, support, and indulgence over the lifespan of this project and to my two wonderful sons, Daniel and Joel, for their ongoing encouragement and support.

References

Center for Behavioral Health Statistics and Quality. 2015. *Behavioral Health Trends in the United States: Results from the 2014 National Survey on Drug Use and Health* (HHS Publication No. SMA 15–4927, NSDUH Series H-50). Retrieved from http://www.samhsa.gov/data/

Dweck, C. 2007. *Mindset: The New Psychology of Success.* New York: Ballantine Books.

Hall, K., and M. H. Cook. 2010. *The Power of Validation: Arming Your Child Against Bullying, Peer Pressure, Addiction, Self-Harm, and Out-of-Control Emotions.* Oakland, CA: New Harbinger Publications.

Honos-Webb, L. 2010. *The Gift of ADHD: How to Transform Your Child's Problems into Strengths.* Oakland, CA: New Harbinger Publications.

Minuchin, S. 1974. *Families and Family Therapy.* Cambridge, MA: Harvard University Press.

Siegel, D. 2014. *Brainstorm: The Power and Purpose of the Teenage Brain.* New York: Penguin Putnam.

Spock, B. 1946. *The Common Sense Book of Baby and Child Care.* New York: Duell, Sloan and Pearce.

Taffel, R., and M. Blau. 2000. *Nurturing Good Children Now: 10 Basic Skills to Protect and Strengthen Your Child's Core Self.* New York: St. Martin's Press.

U.S. Department of Education, National Center for Education Statistics. 2015. *Digest of Education Statistics, 2013* (NCES 2015–011). Retrieved from https://nces.ed.gov/programs/digest /d13/ch_2.asp

Visser, S. N., M. L. Danielson, R. H. Bitsko, J. R. Holbrook, M. D. Kogan, R. N. Ghandour, R. Perou, and S. J. Blumberg. 2014. "Trends in the Parent-Report of Health Care Provider-Diagnosed and Medicated Attention-Deficit/Hyperactivity Disorder: United States, 2003–2011." *Journal of the American Academy of Child and Adolescent Psychiatry.* 53(1):34–46. doi: 0.1016/j.jaac.2013.09.001

Wolf, A. E. 2002. *Get Out of My Life, but First Could You Drive Me and Cheryl to the Mall: A Parent's Guide to the New Teenager, Revised and Updated.* New York: Farrar, Straus and Giroux.

Neil D. Brown, LCSW, is a psychotherapist who has worked with families, couples, and individuals for more than thirty years. Deeply steeped in the theory and practice of family therapy, Brown uses a systemic approach that allows him to understand the system, or context, in which problems are both formed and are healed. This approach has revealed a simple yet profound method of empowering parents and their adolescent youth to put an end to destructive control battles for good. Brown is also a trainer of parents and mental health professionals. Additionally, Brown works in industry with teams and workgroups to increase organizational effectiveness.

Foreword writer Donald T. Saposnek, PhD, is a clinical child psychologist, child custody mediator, and family therapist. As a national and international trainer in mediation and child development, Saposnek has presented hundreds of workshops to judges, lawyers, mediators, and therapists over the past thirty-eight years. Saposnek is adjunct professor at Pepperdine University School of Law's Straus Institute for Dispute Resolution, where he teaches courses in family law mediation and child development. He also teaches on the psychology faculty at the University of California, Santa Cruz.

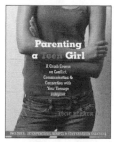

Real change *is* possible

For more than forty-five years, New Harbinger has published proven-effective self-help books and pioneering workbooks to help readers of all ages and backgrounds improve mental health and well-being, and achieve lasting personal growth. In addition, our spirituality books offer profound guidance for deepening awareness and cultivating healing, self-discovery, and fulfillment.

Founded by psychologist Matthew McKay and Patrick Fanning, New Harbinger is proud to be an independent, employee-owned company. Our books reflect our core values of integrity, innovation, commitment, sustainability, compassion, and trust. Written by leaders in the field and recommended by therapists worldwide, New Harbinger books are practical, accessible, and provide real tools for real change.

 **newharbinger**publications